TYCONIUS: THE BOOK OF RULES

Society of Biblical Literature

TEXTS AND TRANSLATIONS

edited by
Robert L. Wilken
William R. Schoedel

Texts and Translations 31
Early Christian Literature Series 7

Tyconius: The Book of Rules

TYCONIUS: THE BOOK OF RULES

Translated,
With an Introduction & Notes

by
William S. Babcock

Scholars Press
Atlanta, Georgia

TYCONIUS: THE BOOK OF RULES

Translated by
William S. Babcock

© 1989
Society of Biblical Literature

Library of Congress Cataloging-in-Publication Data

Tyconius, 4th cent.
  [Liber regularum. English & Latin]
  Tyconius: the book of rules / [edited and translated by] William
S. Babcock.
  p. cm. -- (Texts and translations : 31. Early Christian
literature : 7)
  Latin text and English translation of: Liber regularum.
  Includes index.
  ISBN 1-55540-366-2 (alk. paper). -- ISBN 1-55540-367-0 (pbk. :
alk. paper)
  1. Bible--Hermeneutics. 2. Church--Early works to 1800.
I. Babcock, William S., 1939- II. Title. III. Series: Texts
and translations : no. 31 IV. Series: Texts and translations.
Early Christian literature : 7.
BS476.T5313 1989
220.6'01--dc20
                                                    89-10389
                                                    CIP

Printed in the United States of America
on acid-free paper

Table of Contents

For Michael and Hilary

INTRODUCTION

Tyconius' *Book of Rules* ostensibly consists of seven rules set forth to guide the interpretation of scripture. Like "pathways of light" through a dark forest, the rules will keep the interpreter "from straying into error." Like keys, they will open the "inner recesses" of the biblical text and give access to its hidden depths. It soon becomes clear, however, that the rules are also—and perhaps primarily—the headings under which Tyconius elaborates a remarkable vision of the church as it exists under the conditions of the present era, the period that stretches out between the incarnation on the one hand and the end-time on the other. Or rather, since for Tyconius the incarnation simply makes explicit the dialectic between law and promise that had already been implicit at least from the time of Abraham, it might be better to say that he pictures the church as it has existed from the moment of the promise to Abraham and as it will continue to exist until the second coming of Christ.

For Tyconius, then, Christ has two comings. In the first, he comes not only in his own individual humanity but also and continuously in the form of his body, the church, represented by those who have been saved by faith without reliance on the law or on the works of the law (by which no one is justified). In reading and interpreting scripture, therefore, we must learn—and this is the import of the first rule, "On the Lord and His Body"—to distinguish between those phrases and passages which speak directly of Christ himself and those which speak rather of his body, the church, as it grows through time and spreads throughout the world like the stone that became a great mountain and filled the earth in Daniel 2:35. The church, however, does not represent the body of Christ simply and unambiguously. Mingled with it and part of it are also members of the antithetical body of Satan, made up of those who, like the devil himself, seek to usurp the place of God and to orchestrate human existence as if they themselves were its center. In Tyconius' scheme, antichrist as well as Christ has two comings; and the first is that coming in Satan's body which, because it is marked by the "pretended signs and wonders" of 2 Thessalonians 2:9, looks deceptively like Christ's own first coming in his body, the church. Consequently we must also read and interpret scripture in such a way as to discern when it is speaking of the one and when of the other part of Christ's body (the second rule, "The Lord's Bipartite Body") and must recognize that scripture's discourse about the devil, like its discourse about Christ, slips back and forth between statements about the head and statements about the body (the seventh rule, "The Devil and His Body").

Within the frame established by the dominant imagery of two opposed and yet intermingled bodies, Tyconius also addresses several more specific aspects and questions of biblical interpretation. The third rule, "On the Promises and the Law," serves a double purpose. It supports the Pauline claim that the saved, the true members of Christ's body, are justified by faith and grace quite apart from the law (although, through the gift of the Spirit, they in fact do what the law requires); and it secures the unbroken continuity of the community of the justified through time, both before and after the incarnation, by rooting that continuity in an unconditional and indefeasible divine promise. Because this promise is based on divine foreknowledge of what will take place rather than on divine predestination of who will be saved, however, it still leaves room—and Tyconius is quite explicit on this point—for the workings of human freedom. Tyconius' discussion of these intricately interrelated topics anticipates—although it remains distinctly different from—the interpretation of Paul that Augustine worked out in the years just before he became bishop of Hippo in 396; and Tyconius, like Augustine, deserves to be reckoned among the foremost of the late Latin interpreters of Paul.

The fourth, fifth and sixth rules—"The Particular and the General," "Times," and "Recapitulation"—all deal with particular features of scriptural discourse. In each case, the point is to determine when and how scripture says more or other than it at first appears to say. Under the heading of "The Particular and the General," Tyconius traces the subtle, almost indiscernible patterns in which passages of scripture may oscillate between statements that refer to specific historical persons and events and statements that also or only apply to the wider conditions that obtain throughout the church's existence, and especially to the ongoing, internal opposition between the two parts of Christ's body. In "Times," he explores the meaning of numbers in scripture, giving particular attention to those that designate periods of time. Here he uses the notion that the part can stand for the whole and the whole for the part to resolve certain problems in biblical chronology—the reckoning of the length of the Hebrews' captivity in Egypt and the calculation of the three days and three nights that Christ spent in the tomb—and, more generally, to emphasize that the church's present existence belongs to the era between the incarnation and the end-time, caught in all the ambiguities of its bipartite composition and character. Finally, in "Recapitulation," he shows how biblical descriptions of events happening at one time can also refer to (be recapitulated in) events happening at another. This pattern can move not only forward through time from earlier events to later, but also backwards from later events to earlier; and Tyconius uses it, in particular, to convert descriptions of eschatological happenings into accounts of what is now taking place in the church's life, thus pulling the eschatological future back into the historical present and transforming apocalyptic discourse into hortatory admonition to be on

guard against the immediate inroads of the enemy body in its deviousness and pretence.

The *Book of Rules* ends abruptly, without quite completing the exposition of Ezekiel 28:2-19 that was in progress; and it is impossible to know how Tyconius might have intended to bring his work to a close. Over the entire treatise, however, there hovers the vision of the end-time. Tyconius' eschatology is shaped, in particular, by three biblical passages. The most important is 2 Thessalonians 2:3-10 which, in Tyconius' interpretation (based on his Old Latin biblical text), speaks of a departure "from the midst" when "the mystery of lawlessness" is unleashed. Tyconius associates this departure with Lot's escape from Sodom, just before its destruction, as recounted in Genesis 19 and as cited by Christ, in an apocalyptic context, in Luke 17:28-30; and he construes it as the church's departure from the mixed condition in which it presently exists as the bipartite body of Christ. The end-time, therefore, represents the moment of separation, the moment when the mingled bodies of Christ and Satan are at last untangled and each stands forth in its true character, undiluted and undisguised. Tyconius is usually understood to have expected the imminent end of the world and, in fact, to have calculated its very date within the immediate future. Whether that interpretation is correct or not—and there is good reason to doubt it—it is clear that his vision of the end also has a specifically ecclesiological function: by locating the moment of separation at the end-time, it deliberately cancels any notion that the church might attain pure and unmixed status under the conditions of the present. In the present era, the church always and unavoidably remains the *bipartite* body of Christ.

Tyconius lived and wrote in North Africa in the second half of the fourth century. Of his writings only the *Book of Rules* survives intact or nearly intact. One other, an influential commentary on the Apocalypse, is partially preserved in fragments and in quotations incorporated into later commentaries. It cannot, however, be reconstructed as a whole. In relation to the Donatist controversy, which was certainly the dominant feature on the landscape of North African Christianity in the fourth and early fifth centuries, Tyconius occupied an ambiguous and enigmatic position. He belonged to the Donatist party; but his theology was clearly an anti-Donatist theology. Where the Donatists restricted the legitimate church to their own communion in North Africa, he stressed its spread throughout the world. Where they insisted on a purified church, uncompromised and uncompromising in its alienation from the social and political orders, he portrayed a mixed community comprised at once of the body of Christ and the body of Satan. Where they sought rigorous separation of true Christians and false Christians, he reserved the untangling of true and false for Christ's second coming at the end of time. It is little wonder, then, that Tyconius was repudiated by a Donatist council in the 380's or that his theology should have seemed more attractive to the catholic Augustine than it did to his fellow

Donatists. Augustine took up, modified and developed both the exegetical rules and the ecclesiological vision of the *Book of Rules* (see in particular—but by no means exclusively—Augustine's *De doctrina christiana* 3.30.42–37.56); and he used them, among other things, to formulate a catholic response to the Donatist challenge. Although Tyconius did not himself become a catholic Christian, he may be considered—ironically enough—the first architect of the theology that would, in Augustine's hands, defeat the Donatism he never fully rejected and shape the catholic tradition he never finally accepted.

Bibliographical Note

For an older but still useful general treatment of Tyconius' life, thought and writings, see Pierre Monceaux, *Histoire Littéraire de l'Afrique Chrétienne* (Paris, 1920) 5: 165-219. Still basic to any study of Tyconius is Traugot Hahn, *Tyconius-Studien* (Leipzig, 1900). The now classic work on Donatism is W. H. C. Frend, *The Donatist Church* (Oxford, 1952). On Tyconius' view of the church, there is Joseph Ratzinger, "Beobachtungen zum Kirchenbegriff des Tyconius im *Liber Regularum*," *Revue des études augustiniennes* 2 (1956): 173-185; and on the relation of Tyconius to Augustine with respect to the interpretation of Paul and the doctrine of grace, see Alberto Pincherle, "Da Ticonio a Sant' Augustino," *Richerche Religiose* 1 (1925): 443-466 and my articles "Augustine and Tyconius: A Study in the Latin Appropriation of Paul," *Studia Patristica* 17 (1982): 1209-1215 and "Augustine's Interpretation of Romans (A.D. 394-396)," *Augustinian Studies* 10 (1979): 55-74. An effective counter to the prevailing view that Tyconius expected the imminent end of the world is provided in Paula Fredriksen Landes, "Tyconius and the End of the World," *Revue des études augustiniennes* 28 (1982): 59-75. For a good recent summary of what is known of Tyconius' life and works, see André Mandouze, *Prosopographie chrétienne du Bas-Empire*, vol. 1: *Prosopographie de l'Afrique chrétienne (303-533)* (Paris, 1982), 1122-1127. On the commentary on the Apocalypse, there is now Kenneth B. Steinhauser, *The Apocalypse Commentary of Tyconius: A History of its Reception and Influence* (Frankfurt am Main, Bern, and New York, 1987) which includes a brief discussion of the *Book of Rules* and its relation to the commentary. A more extensive treatment of the *Book of Rules* can be found in Pamela Bright, *The Book of Rules of Tyconius: Its Purpose and Inner Logic* (Notre Dame, IN, 1988) and of the sixth rule in particular in Steinhauser, "*Recapitulatio* in Tyconius and Augustine," *Augustinian Studies* 15 (1984): 1-5. The questions of interpretation, however, are delicate and difficult; and none of the issues appear to be closed.

The Text

The Latin text of the *Book of Rules* reprinted here is that established by F. C. Burkitt and published in his *The Book of Rules of Tyconius*, Texts and Studies 3:1 (Cambridge, 1894). Burkitt's introduction to this volume discusses the surviving manuscripts and reviews the printed editions of Tyconius' work. In addition, it offers an extensive study of the text of Tyconius' Latin Bible. I have departed from Burkitt's text of the *Book of Rules* at only one point, which is duly noted in a footnote registering the alternate reading I have adopted. I have altered Burkitt's paragraphing, however, when it seemed that such alterations would help to clarify the patterns of Tyconius' thought and argument; and I have deviated from his practice by introducing capitals at the beginning of sentences and, in the area of orthography, by substituting *im-* for *in-* and *v* for the consonantal *u*. These changes will, I hope, make it easier to work with the Latin text. Finally, in translating Tyconius' scriptural quotations, I have tried to use language that retains some resonance—or even, where possible, the very phrasing—of the Revised Standard Version, which is probably still the most widely familiar English translation of the Bible; but I have made no attempt to force Tyconius' old Latin biblical text into consistent or systematic conformity with any modern English translation of scripture.

Acknowledgements

I wish gratefully to acknowledge the permission granted by Cambridge University Press to reprint Burkitt's text of the *Book of Rules*. In addition, I want to express my appreciation to my former colleague Harold W. Attridge, now at the University of Notre Dame, for help with one or two particularly puzzling passages. Above all, I am grateful to Mary Ann Marshall who typed the English translation through all my corrections and revisions with unfailing accuracy, patience, and good humor and to Eugene H. Lovering, Jr., then a student in Southern Methodist University's Graduate Program in Religious Studies, who typed the Latin text with infinite care and compiled the scripture index. In another capacity, he has now readied the entire work for the press. Robert L. Wilken and William R. Schoedel, the editors of the Early Christian Literature Series, read the translation carefully and critically at the stage when it most needed an outside eye. To them also I owe thanks; such flaws as remain are my mistakes, not theirs.

LIBER REGULARUM TYCONII

TYCONIUS' BOOK OF RULES

LIBER REGULARUM TYCONII

Necessarium duxi ante omnia quae mihi videntur libellum regularem scribere, et secretorum legis veluti claves et luminaria fabricare. Sunt enim quaedam regulae mysticae quae universae legis recessus obtinent et veritatis thesauros aliquibus invisibiles faciunt; quarum si ratio regularum sine invidia ut communicamus accepta fuerit, clausa quaeque patefient et obscura dilucidabuntur, ut quis prophetiae immensam silvam perambulans his regulis quodam modo lucis tramitibus deductus ab errore defendatur.

Sunt autem regulae istae:

I. De Domino et corpore eius.
II. De Domini corpore bipertito.
III. De promissis et lege.
IV. De specie et genere.
V. De temporibus.
VI. De recapitulatione.
VII. De diabolo et eius corpore.

I. De Domino et corpore eius

Dominum eiusne corpus, id est Ecclesiam, Scriptura loquatur, sola ratio discernit, dum quid cui conveniat persuadet vel quia tanta est vis veritatis extorquet.

Alias una persona conuenitur quam duplicem esse diversa duorum officia edocent. Sic per Esaiam: *Hic* inquit *peccata nostra feret et pro nobis dolet, ipse vulneratus est propter facinora nostra, et Deus tradidit eum pro peccatis nostris*, et cetera quae in Dominum convenire omnis Ecclesiae ore celebratur. Sequitur autem et dicit de eodem: *Et Deus vult purgare illum a plaga et vult Deus a dolore auferre animam eius, ostendere illi lucem et formare illum prudentia.* Numquid ei quem *tradidit pro peccatis nostris vult ostendere lucem*, et eum *formare prudentia*, cum ipse sit lux et sapientia Dei, et non corpori eius? Qua re manifestum est sola ratione videri posse quando a capite ad corpus transitum facit.

TYCONIUS' BOOK OF RULES

Above everything else that came to mind, I considered it necessary to write a book of rules and so to fashion keys and lamps, as it were, to the secrets of the law. For there are certain mystic rules which obtain in the inner recesses of the entire law and keep the rich treasures of the truth hidden from some people. But if the sense of these rules is accepted without ill will, as we impart it, whatever is closed will be opened and whatever is dark will be illumined; and anyone who walks the vast forest of prophecy guided by these rules, as by pathways of light, will be kept from straying into error.

These are the rules:

    I. The Lord and His Body
   II. The Lord's Bipartite Body
  III. The Promises and the Law
  IV. The Particular and the General
   V. Times
  VI. Recapitulation
 VII. The Devil and His Body

I. The Lord and His Body

Whether scripture is speaking about the Lord or about his body, i.e., the church, reason alone discerns, persuading or, such is the force of truth, compelling us to recognize what pertains to each.

In some cases, the subject is a single person; and yet the different functions of the two teach us that the one person is actually twofold. Thus in Isaiah, it says: "he bears our sins and knows sorrow on our behalf; he was wounded for our iniquities and God delivered him up for our sins," and so forth[1]—a passage which the voice of the church universally ascribes to the Lord. But it goes on to say, still speaking of the same person: "and God wishes to free him from affliction, and God wishes to take away his sorrow, to show him the light and to form him with prudence."[2] Does God "wish to show the light" to the same one whom "he delivered up for our sins" or wish "to form him with prudence," especially when that one is himself the very light and wisdom of God? Do not these phrases apply rather to his body? From this it is clear that only reason can tell when there is a transition from the head to the body.

---

[1] Is. 53:4, 5, 6
[2] Is. 53:10, 11

Danihel quoque *lapidem de monte praecisum* et *impegisse* in corpus regnorum mundi et *in pulverem commoluisse* Dominum dicet, *montem* vero *effectum et implevisse universam terram* corpus eius. Non enim—sicut quidam dicunt in contumeliam regni Dei invictaeque hereditatis Christi, quod non sine dolore dico—Dominus totum mundum potestate et non sui corporis plenitudine occupavit. Dicunt enim eo monte mundum impletum, quod liceat Christiano in omni loco, quod antea non nisi in Sion licebat offerre. Quod si ita est, non opus erat dicere ex lapide montem effectum et incrementis mundum cepisse. Dominus enim noster Christus *ante mundi constitutionem hanc habuit claritatem*, et cum homo in illo Dei filius fieret non paulatim ut lapis sed uno tempore accepit omnem potestatem in caelo et in terra. Lapis autem incrementis *factus est mons magnus* et crescendo terram omnem texit. Quod si potestate implesset universam terram non corpore, lapidi non compararetur. Potestas res est impalpabilis, lapis vero corpus palpabile.

Nec sola ratione manifestatur corpus non caput crescere, sed etiam apostolica auctoritate firmatur: *Crescimus* inquit *per omnia in eum qui est caput, Christus, ex quo omne corpus constructum et conexum per omnem tuctum subministrationis in mensuram unius cuiusque partis incrementum corporis facit in aedificationem sui.* Et iterum: *Non tenens caput, ex quo omne corpus per tactus et coniunctiones constructum et subministratum crescit in incrementum Dei.* Non ergo caput, quod ex origine idem est, sed corpus crescit ex capite.

Ad propositum redeamus. Scriptum est de Domino et eius corpore—quid cui conveniat ratione discernendum—: *Angelis suis mandavit de te ut custodiant te in omnibus viis tuis, in manibus ferant te ne offendas ad lapidem pedem tuum. Super aspidem et basiliscum ambulabis, et conculcabis leonem et draconem. Quoniam in me speravit eripiam eum, protegam illum quoniam cognovit nomen meum. Invocabit me et exaudiam eum, cum ipso sum in tribulatione, eripiam et glorificabo eum. Longitudinem dierum adimplebo eum et ostendam illi salutare meum.*

Daniel, too, calls the Lord "a stone cut from the mountain" and says that he "struck" the body of the kingdoms of the world and "ground it into dust," but that his own body "became a mountain and filled the whole earth."[1] For it is not that the Lord filled the whole earth with his power rather than with the fullness of his body. Some make this claim—which I do not report without sorrow—to the dishonor of God's kingdom and of Christ's unvanquished inheritance.[2] They maintain that the world is filled by the mountain because a Christian may now rightly offer in every place what before was rightly offered only in Sion. But if this is so, there was no need to say that the mountain grew from the stone and took possession of the world by degrees. For Christ our Lord "had this glory before the foundation of the world";[3] and when the son of God became man in him, he did not receive all power in heaven and on earth little by little like the stone, but all at once. The stone, in contrast, "became a great mountain" by degrees and covered the whole earth by its increase. Furthermore, if he had filled the whole earth not with his body but with his power, he would not be compared to a stone. Power is intangible; but a stone is a tangible body.

Nor is reason alone in showing that the body grows, not the head. This point is also confirmed by apostolic authority: "we are growing in every way into him who is the head, Christ, from whom the whole body, fitted and joined together through every operation supplied according to the measure of each part, makes bodily increase towards building itself up."[4] And again: "not holding fast to the head, from whom the whole body, fitted and furnished in its joints and operations, grows into God's increase."[5] The head, therefore, does not grow; it is the same from the beginning. Rather the body takes its growth from the head.

Let us return to our thesis. Of the Lord and his body—and reason must discern what pertains to each—it is written: "he charged his angels to guard you in all your ways, to take you in their hands lest you should strike your foot against a stone. You will tread on the asp and the basilisk, and will trample the lion and the serpent under foot. Because he put his hope in me, I will rescue him; I will protect him because he knows my name. He will call upon me and I will heed him; I am with him in tribulation; I will rescue and honor him. I will lengthen his days and show him my salvation."[6] Does God "show his salvation" to

---

[1]Dan. 2:34-35

[2]Tyconius, it appears, is attacking the Donatist claim that the true Church (Christ's body) is found only in North Africa in the Donatist communion itself and therefore can fill the earth only in some metaphorical sense.

[3]Jn. 17:5, 24

[4]Eph. 4:15-16

[5]Col. 2:19

[6]Ps. 91:11-16

Numquid de cuius obsequio *mandavit angelis suis* Deus eidem ostendit salutare suum, et non corpori eius?

Iterum: *Sicut sponso imposuit mihi mitram et sicut sponsam ornavit me ornamento.* Unum corpus dixit utriusque sexus sponsi et sponsae, sed quid in Dominum quid in Ecclesiam conveniat ratione cognoscitur. Et idem Dominus dicit in Apocalypsi: *Ego sum sponsus et sponsa.* Et iterum: *Exierunt obviam sponso et sponsae.*

Et iterum quid capitis quid corporis ratione discernendum sit per Esaiam declaratur: *Sic dicit Dominus Christo meo Domino cuius ego tenui dexteram ut exaudiant eum gentes*—sequitur et dicit quod non nisi corpori conveniat—*et dabo tibi thesauros absconditos, invisibiles aperiam tibi, ut scias quoniam ego sum Dominus qui voco nomen tuum Deus Israhel, propter Iacob puerum meum et Israhel electum meum.* Propter testamenta enim quae disposuit patribus ad cognoscendum se Deus aperit corpori Christi thesauros invisibiles, *quod oculus non vidit nec auris audivit nec in cor hominis ascendit*, sed obdurati hominis qui non est in corpore Christi; Ecclesiae *autem revelavit Deus per Spiritum suum.* Ista quidem, quamvis hoc quoque Dei gratia sit, adhibita tamen ratione aliquando facilius videntur.

Sunt alia in quibus huiusmodi ratio minus claret, eo quod sive in Dominum sive in corpus eius recte conveniat dictum; quam ob rem sola et maiore Dei gratia videri possunt. Sic in Evangelio: *A modo* inquit *videbitis filium hominis sedentem ad dexteram virtutis et venientem in nubibus caeli.* Alio loco dicit non visuros venientem in nubibus caeli nisi in novissimo tantum die: *Plangent se omnes tribus terrae, et tunc videbunt filium hominis venientem in nubibus caeli.* Utrumque autem fieri necesse est, sed primo corporis est adventus, id est Ecclesiae, iugiter venientis in eadem claritate invisibili, deinde capitis, id est Domini, in manifesta claritate. Si enim diceret Modo videbitis venientem, solius corporis

the same one whose care he has "charged" to "his angels"—or rather to his body?

Again: "he has put a wreath on my head like a bridegroom and has adorned me with jewels like a bride."[1]   He speaks of one body of both sexes, bridegroom and bride; but by reason we know what pertains to the Lord, what to the church. And in the Apocalypse the same Lord says: "I am the bridegroom and the bride."[2]   And again: "they went to meet the bridegroom and the bride."[3]

And again it is made clear in Isaiah that reason must discern what has to do with the head, what with the body: "thus says the Lord to Christ my Lord, whose right hand I have taken that the nations might heed him"—and it goes on to say what can only pertain to the body— "and I will give you hidden treasures, things unseen I will disclose to you, that you may know that I am the Lord, the God of Israel, who calls your name, for the sake of Jacob my servant and Israel my chosen one."[4] For the sake of the covenants[5] which he established with the fathers so that they should know him, God discloses to the body of Christ unseen treasures, "what eye has not seen, nor ear heard, nor the heart of man conceived"—but this is the hardened man who does not belong to the body of Christ; to the church, however, "God has revealed" it "through his Spirit."[6] Such things, although this too is God's grace, are sometimes seen more easily when set forth by reason.

There are other cases in which reasoning of this kind is less clear, since what is said applies appropriately whether referred to the Lord or to his body. Consequently they can be understood only with the greater grace of God. Thus in the gospel he says: "from this moment you will see the son of man sitting at the right hand of power and coming on the clouds of heaven."[7] In another passage, however, he says that they will not see him coming on the clouds of heaven until the last day: "all the tribes of earth will mourn, and then they will see the son of man coming on the clouds of heaven."[8] Both comings must take place; but first there is the advent of the body, i.e., the church, which comes continuously in the same invisible glory, then the advent of the head, i.e., the Lord, in manifest glory. If he had said, "now you will see him coming,"

---

[1]Is. 61:10

[2]Rev. 22:16, 17

[3]Mt. 25:1

[4]Is. 45:1, 3-4

[5]The plural "covenants" is perhaps a reminiscence of Rom 9:4, a verse of which Tyconius later makes explicit use (below, p. 49).

[6]1 Cor. 2:9, 10

[7]Mt. 26:64

[8]Mt. 24:30. The contrast between the two Matthean passages, in Tyconius' view, is the contrast between "from now on" ("from this moment") and "not until."

intellegendus esset adventus; si autem Videbitis, capitis adventus. Nunc vero *A modo* inquit *videbitis venientem*, quoniam corpore suo iugiter venit nativitate et similium passionum claritate.　Si enim renati Christi membra efficiuntur et membra corpus efficiunt, Christus est qui venit, quoniam nativitas adventus est sicut scriptum est: *Illuminat omnem hominem venientem in hunc mundum.* Et iterum: *Generatio vadit et generatio venit.* Et iterum: *Sicut audistis quia antichristus venit.* Iterum de eodem corpore: *Si enim iste qui venit alium Iesum praedicat.* Unde Dominus cum de signo adventus sui interrogaretur, de illo adventu suo coepit disputare qui ab inimico corpore signis et prodigiis imitari potest. *Cavete* inquit *ne quis vos seducat; multi enim venient in nomine meo,* id est in nomine corporis mei.　Novissimo autem adventu Domini, id est consummationis et manifestationis totius adventus eius, nemo ut aliqui putant mentietur. Sed quo plenius ista dicantur ordini suo relinquimus.

　　Nec illud erit absurdum quod ex uno totum corpus volumus intellegi, ut filium hominis Ecclesiam; quoniam Ecclesia, id est filii Dei redacti in unum corpus, dicti sunt filius Dei, dicti unus homo, dicti etiam Deus sicut per apostolum: *Super omne qui dicitur Deus aut quod colitur—qui dicitur Deus* Ecclesia est, *quod* autem *colitur* Deus summus est—*ut in templum Dei*

the advent of the body alone would have to be understood; if "you will see," the advent of the head. But in fact he says, "from this moment you will see him coming," since he comes continuously in his body through its birth and through its glory in sufferings like his own. For if those who are reborn become members of Christ and the members make up the body, then it is Christ who comes, since birth is a form of advent, as it is written: "he enlightens every man who comes into this world."[1] And again: "a generation goes and a generation comes."[2] And again: "as you have heard that antichrist is coming."[3] Again, with reference to the same body: "for if the one who comes preaches another Jesus."[4] Thus, when the Lord was asked about the sign of his coming, he began to talk about that advent of his which the enemy body can imitate with signs and wonders.[5] "Be on guard," he said, "lest anyone lead you astray; for many will come in my name,"[6] i.e., in the name of my body. In contrast—whatever some may think—no one will speak falsely at the Lord's final advent, i.e., at the consummation and manifestation of his full advent. But we leave a fuller discussion of such matters to its proper place.

Nor is it absurd that we want the whole body to be represented in a single individual, for example, the church in the son of man.[7] For the church, i.e., the children of God gathered into one body, is called "son of God"; it is called "one man"; it is even called "God," as we find in the apostle: "above everything that is called God or that is worshiped"—that "which is called God" is the church, and that "which is worshiped" is the supreme God—"so that he takes his seat in the temple of God,

---

[1] Jn. 1:9

[2] Eccles. 1:4

[3] 1 Jn. 2:18. Here, without warning, Tyconius slides over from the theme of the continuous coming of Christ in his body, the church, to the antithetical theme of the continuous coming of the devil in his body (on which see below, n. 5). It is thus the devil's body that, as the following sentences indicate, may preach "another Christ" or, "with signs and wonders," imitate the coming of Christ's body.

[4] 2 Cor. 11:4

[5] The theme of the enemy body, i.e., the devil and his body, opposite although not quite equal to Christ and his body, becomes gradually more prominent in *The Book of Rules* and is treated at length in the seventh rule. The present sentence contains an allusion to 2 Thess. 2:9 which, together with the surrounding verses, is a crucial text for Tyconius' eschatology.

[6] Mt. 24:4-5

[7] Tyconius is still thinking, here, of the church as represented by the son of man coming continuously on the clouds of heaven. What follows in the next several paragraphs is a sequence of examples designed to show how, in scripture, names or titles properly belonging to one person are used to designate an entire group and especially the group that makes up the body of Christ, i.e., the church.

sedeat ostendens se quod ipse est Deus, id est quod ipse sit Ecclesia. Quale si diceret: *in templum Dei sedeat ostendens se* quod ipse sit Dei templum, aut: in Deum sedeat *ostendens se quod ipse* sit *Deus.* Sed hunc intellectum synonymis voluit obscurare.

Danihel de rege novissimo *in Deum* inquit *locus eius glorificabitur,* id est clarificabitur; veluti Ecclesiam in loco Ecclesiae, *in loco sancto, abominationem vastationis* in Deum, id est in Ecclesiam, subornabit. Et Dominus totum populum *sponsam* dicit et *sororem*; et apostolus *virginem sanctam,* et adversum corpus *hominem peccati.* Et David totam Ecclesiam Christum dicit: *Faciens misericordias Christo suo David et semini eius in aeternum.* Et apostolus Paulus corpus Christi Christum appellat dicens: *Sicut enim corpus unum est, membra autem habet multa, omnia autem membra ex uno corpore cum sint multa unum corpus est, sic et Christus,* id est Christi corpus quod est Ecclesia. Iterum: *Gaudeo in passionibus pro vobis et repleo quae desunt pressurarum Christi,* id est Ecclesiae. Nihil enim defuit Christi passionibus, quoniam *sufficit discipulo ut sit sicut magister.* Sic ergo *adventum Christi* pro locis accipiemus.

Item in Exodo omnes filios Dei unum filium et omnes primogenitos Aegypti unum primogenitum esse sic Deo dicente cognoscimus. *Dices* inquit *Pharaoni: Haec dicit Dominus, Filius meus primitivus Israhel. Dixi autem, Dimitte populum ut serviat mihi; tu autem noluisti dimittere eum. Vide ergo, ecce ego occido filium tuum primitivum.* Et David vineam Domini unum filium sic ait: *Deus virtutum convertere, respice de caelo et vide, visita vineam tuam. Et perfice eam quam plantavit dextera tua et in filium corroborasti tibi.*

claiming that he is himself God,"[1] i.e., that he is himself the church. He might just as well have said: "he takes his seat in the temple of God, claiming that he is himself" the temple of God; or: he takes his seat in God, "claiming that he is himself God." But the apostle wanted to obscure this interpretation by using synonymous phrases.

Speaking of the final king, Daniel says that "his place will be exalted," i.e., magnified, "above God."[2] Like a church in the church's place, "in the holy place," he will install "the abomination of desolation"[3] in God, i.e., in the church. The Lord also calls the whole people his "bride" and his "sister";[4] and the apostle calls them a "holy virgin"[5] and speaks of the enemy body as "the man of sin."[6] David, too, calls the whole church "Christ": "showing mercy to his Christ, to David and his descendants for ever."[7] And the apostle Paul calls the body of Christ "Christ" when he says: "for just as the body is one, though it has many members, and all the members of one body, though many, make one body, so it is with Christ,"[8] i.e., the body of Christ which is the church. Again: "I rejoice in my sufferings for your sake and I complete what is lacking in the afflictions of Christ,"[9] i.e., of the church. For nothing was lacking in Christ's sufferings, since "it is enough for the disciple to be like his teacher."[10] So it is, therefore, that we must interpret Christ's coming according to the context.

Likewise in Exodus, where God speaks in similar fashion, we know that the one son means all the sons of God and the one first-born all the first-born of Egypt: "you will say to Pharaoh: Thus says the Lord, Israel is my first-born son. I have said, let the people go that they may serve me; but you refuse to let them go. Take note therefore, I will kill your first born son."[11] David also speaks of the Lord's vine as one son in this way: "turn again, God of hosts, look down from heaven and see, have regard for your vine. Make perfect that which you planted with your right hand and made strong as a son for yourself."[12]

---

[1]2 Thess. 2:4

[2]Dan. 11:36

[3]Mt. 24:15

[4]Song 5:1

[5]2 Cor. 11:2

[6]2 Thess. 2:3

[7]Ps. 18:50

[8]1 Cor. 12:12

[9]Col. 1:24

[10]Mt. 10:25

[11]Ex. 4:22-23

[12]Ps. 80:14-15

Et apostolus filium Dei dicit qui filio Dei mixtus est: *Paulus servus Iesu Christi, vocatus apostolus, segregatus in evangelium Dei quod ante promiserat per prophetas suos in scripturis sanctis de filio suo, qui factus est ei ex semine David secundum carnem, qui praedestinatus est filius Dei in virtute secundum Spiritum sanctitatis ex resurrectione mortuorum Iesu Christi Domini nostri.* Si diceret *de filio suo ex resurrectione mortuorum,* unum filium ostenderat; nunc autem *de filio* inquit *suo ex resurrectione mortuorum Iesu Christi Domini nostri.* Sed *qui factus est filius Dei ex resurrectione Christi* apertius ostendit dicens *de filio qui factus est ei ex semine David secundum carnem, qui praedestinatus est filius Dei.* Dominus autem noster non est Dei filius praedestinatus (quia Deus est et coaequalis est Patri) qui ex quo natus est hoc est, sed ille cui secundum Lucam dicit in baptismo: *Filius meus es tu, ego hodie generavi te.* Qui *ex semine David,* mixtus est *principali Spiritui* et *factus est* ipse *filius Dei ex resurrectione Domini nostri Iesu Christi,* id est dum resurgit in Christo semen David; non ille de quo ait ipse David: *Sic dicit Dominus Domino meo.*

Itaque facti sunt duo una caro. *Verbum caro factum est* et caro Deus, quia *non ex sanguine sed ex Deo nati sumus.* Apostolus dicit: *Erunt duo in carne una. Sacramentum hoc magnum est, ego autem dico in Christum et in Ecclesiam.* Unum namque semen promisit Deus Abrahae, ut quanticumque Christo miscerentur unus esset in Christo, sicut Apostolus dicit: *Omnes vos unus estis in Christo Iesu. Si autem vos unus estis in Christo Iesu, ergo Abrahae semen estis et secundum promissionem heredes.* Distat autem inter *unum estis* et *unus estis.* Quotienscumque alter alteri voluntate miscetur *unum* sunt, sicut Dominus dicit: *Ego et pater unum sumus.* Quotiens autem et corporaliter miscentur et in unam carnem duo solidantur *unus* sunt.

Corpus itaque in capite suo filius est Dei, et Deus in corpore suo filius est hominis, qui cotidie nascendo venit et crescit in templum sanctum Dei.

The apostle, too, calls the one who was united to the son of God "the son of God": "Paul, a servant of Jesus Christ, called to be an apostle, set apart for the gospel of God which he had promised beforehand through his prophets in the holy scriptures, the gospel concerning his son who was descended from David according to the flesh, who was predestined as son of God in power according to the Spirit of holiness by the resurrection from the dead of Jesus Christ our Lord."[1] If he had said, "concerning his son by the resurrection from the dead," he would have indicated one son only. But, in fact, he said "concerning his son by the resurrection from the dead of Jesus Christ our Lord." And he plainly shows us who it was "who became son of God by the resurrection of Christ," when he says: "concerning his son who was descended from David according to the flesh, who was predestined as son of God." Our Lord, since he is God and coequal with the Father, is not the predestined son of God, who is predestined son only after his birth. The predestined son is rather the one to whom, in Luke, he says at his baptism: "you are my son, today I have begotten you."[2] The one "who was descended from David" was united to "the prime Spirit."[3] And he—rather than the one of whom David himself says, "the Lord says to my Lord"[4]—is the one who "became son of God by the resurrection of our Lord Jesus Christ," i.e., when David's descendant rose in Christ.

And so the two became one flesh. "The Word became flesh" and the flesh God, for we are "born not of blood but of God."[5] The apostle says: "the two will be in one flesh. This is a great mystery, and I am saying that it refers to Christ and the church."[6] For God promised one offspring to Abraham, so that, however many are united to Christ, they will be one in Christ. As the apostle says, "you are all one in Christ Jesus. And if you are one in Christ Jesus, then you are Abraham's offspring and heirs according to the promise."[7] Moreover there is a difference between "you are at one" [unum estis] and "you are one" [unus estis]. When one person is united to another by a common will, they are "at one," as the Lord says, "I and my father are at one."[8] But when they are also united in body and the two are compacted into one flesh, they are "one."

And so the body, in virtue of its head, is the son of God; and God, in virtue of his body, is the son of man who comes daily by birth and

---

[1]Rom. 1:1-4
[2]Lk. 3:22
[3]Ps. 51:12
[4]Ps. 110:1
[5]Jn. 1:14, 13
[6]Eph. 5:31-32
[7]Gal. 3:28-29 (cf. Gal. 3:16)
[8]Jn. 10:30

Templum enim bipertitum est, cuius pars altera quamvis lapidibus magnis extruatur destruitur, neque in eo *lapis super lapidem relinquitur.* Istius nobis iugis aduentus cavendus est, *donec de medio* eius discedat Ecclesia.

II. De Domini corpore bipertito.

Regula bipertiti corporis Domini multo necessarior et a nobis tanto diligentius perspicienda et per omnes Scripturas ante oculos habenda est. Sicut enim ut supradictum est a capite ad corpus ratione sola videtur, ita a parte corporis ad partem, a dextera ad sinistram vel a sinistra ad dexteram, transitus reditusque ut in supradicto capite claret.

Dum enim dicit uni corpori: *Thesauros invisibiles aperiam tibi, ut scias quoniam ego sum Dominus, et assumam te,* et adiecit: *Tu autem me non cognovisti quoniam ego sum Deus et non est absque me Deus, et nesciebas me;* numquid licet unum corpus adloquatur in unam mentem convenit *thesauros invisibiles aperiam tibi, ut cognoscas quia ego sum Deus propter puerum meum Iacob,* et *tu autem me non cognovisti?* In eandem et non accepit Iacob quod Deus promisit? Aut in unam mentem convenit *tu autem me non cognovisti* et *nesciebas me? Nesciebas* enim non dicitur nisi ei qui iam scit, *non cognovisti* autem illi dicitur qui, licet ad hoc vocatus sit ut cognosceret, et eiusdem corporis sit visibiliter, et Deo *labiis adpropinquet, corde tamen longe separatus* sit. Huic dicit *tu autem me non cognovisti.*

"grows into the holy temple of God."[1] For the temple is bipartite; and its other part, although it is being constructed with great blocks of stone, will be destroyed and "not one stone will be left upon another."[2] Against the continuous coming of that temple we must remain on guard until the church shall depart "from the midst"[3] of it.

II. The Lord's Bipartite Body

Far more necessary is the rule concerning the bipartite character of the Lord's body; and so we must examine it all the more carefully, keeping it before our eyes through all the scriptures. For just as the transition from head to body and back again, as indicated above, is only seen by reason, so also reason alone sees the transition and return from one part of the body to the other, from the right-hand part to the left or from the left to the right, as was clear in the previous section.

For when he tells the one body, "unseen treasures I will disclose to you, that you may know that I am the Lord, and I will take you to myself," he adds, "but you do not know me, that I am God and there is no other God besides me, and you were ignorant of me."[4] He is speaking to the one body; but do both phrases—"unseen treasures I will open to you, that you may know that I am God, for the sake of Jacob my servant," and, "but you do not know me"—refer to a single mind? Did Jacob, with one and the same mind, both receive and not receive God's promise? Or again, do both, "but you do not know me" and "you were ignorant of me," apply to the same mind? "You were ignorant" is an expression used only in speaking to someone who now knows; but "you do not know" is addressed to the person who "draws near to God with his lips, yet is far from him in his heart,"[5] even though he was called precisely to know and, visibly speaking, belongs to exactly the same body. It is to this person that he says, "but you do not know me."

---

[1]Eph. 2:21. The reference to the "holy temple of God" again suggests to Tyconius the antithetical theme of the unholy temple which, like the church in the body of Christ, also comes continuously and against whose coming the church must constantly be on guard. More precisely, as the second rule will show, it suggests the notion that the temple itself, i.e., the body of Christ, is bipartite, holy in one part and unholy in the other. The unholy part is, in Tyconius' thought, identified with the "enemy body." But the two parts will not be separated until the end-time when the church (the holy part) will depart from the midst of it (the unholy part). Until then the body of Christ will remain bipartite, both holy and unholy. Once again Tyconius is tacitly arguing against the Donatists' claim to have separated the true church from the false already and to have identified the true church with their own communion

[2]Mt. 24:2

[3]2 Thess. 2:7

[4]Is. 45:3, 4, 5. See above, p. 7, for previous discussion of this passage.

[5]Is. 29:13

Iterum: *Ducam caecos in viam quam non noverunt, et semitas quas non noverunt calcabunt, et faciam illis tenebras in lucem et prava in directum. Haec verba faciam et non derelinquam eos. Ipsi autem conversi sunt retro.* Numquid quos dixit *non derelinquam* idem conversi sunt retro, et non pars eorum?

Iterum dicit Dominus ad Iacob: *Noli metuere quia tecum sum. Ab Oriente adducam semen tuum et ab Occidente colligam te. Dicam Aquiloni adduc, et Africo noli vetare; adduc filios meos de terra longinqua et filias meas a summo terrae, omnes in quibus vocatum est nomen meum. In gloria enim mea paravi illum et finxi et feci illum, et produxi plebem caecam, et oculi eorum sunt similiter caeci et surdas aures habent.* Numquid quos in gloriam suam paravit idem sunt caeci et surdi?

Iterum: *Patres tui primo et principes eorum facinus admiserunt in me et inquinaverunt principes tui sancta mea, et dedi perire Iacob, et Israhel in maledictum. Nunc audi me puer meus Iacob, et Israhel quem elegi.* Ostendit illum Iacob dedisse perire et Israhel maledictum quem non elegerat.

Iterum: *Finxi te puerum meum, meus es tu Israhel, noli oblivisci mei. Ecce enim delevi velut nubem facinora tua et sicut nimbum peccata tua. Convertere ad me et redimam te.* Numquid cuius peccata delevit, cui dicit *meus es tu* et ne sui obliviscatur commemorat, eidem dicit *convertere ad me?* Aut alicuius antequam convertatur peccata delentur?

Iterum: *Scio quoniam reprobatus reprobaberis; propter nomen meum ostendam tibi dignitatem meam, et praeclara mea superducam tibi.* Numquid reprobato ostendit dignitatem suam et praeclara inducit ei?

Iterum: *Non senior non angelus, sed ipse conservavit eos, propter quod diligeret eos et parceret illis; ipse redemit eos et assumsit illos et exaltavit illos omnes dies saeculi. Ipsi autem contumaces fuerunt et exacerbaverunt*

Again: "I will lead the blind in a way they do not know; and they will tread paths they do not know; and I will turn the darkness into light for them and make the crooked straight. I will do what I say, and I will not forsake them. But they have been turned back."[1] Are those who have been turned back the same ones of whom he said "I will not forsake them"—and not rather a part of them?

Again the Lord says to Jacob: "do not be afraid, for I am with you. I will bring your offspring from the east, and from the west I will gather you. I will say to the north, bring them up, and to the south, do not forbid them. Bring back my sons from far away and my daughters from the end of the earth, all among whom my name is invoked. For I fashioned him in my glory, and I formed and made him, and I have brought forth a blind people, and their eyes too are blind, and they have deaf ears."[2] Are the blind and the deaf the same ones whom he fashioned in his glory?

Again: "At the first your fathers and their princes committed a crime against me, and your princes defiled my sanctuary, and I gave Jacob to destruction and Israel to the curse. Now listen to me, Jacob my servant, and Israel whom I have chosen."[3] He shows us that the Jacob he gave to destruction, the Israel who was cursed, was the Jacob he had not chosen.[4]

Again: "I formed you as my servant, you are mine, Israel; do not forget me. For, behold, I have swept away your crimes like a cloud and your sins like a mist. Turn to me and I will redeem you."[5] Is the one whose sins he has swept away, to whom he says, "you are mine," and whom he reminds not to forget him, the same one to whom he says, "turn to me"? Are anyone's sins swept away before he is turned?

Again: "I know that as one rejected you will be rejected. For my name's sake I will show you my greatness and will draw my excellence over you."[6] Does he show his greatness to the rejected or wrap him in his excellence?

Again: "It was not an elder nor an angel, but he himself who saved them, because he loved them and pitied them; he himself redeemed them and lifted them up and exalted them all the days of their life. But they were rebellious, and they grieved the Holy Spirit."[7] If he exalted them

---

[1]Is. 42:16-17

[2]Is. 43:5-8

[3]Is. 43:27-44:1

[4]For the double significance of Jacob in Tyconius' view, see below, pp. 51-53.

[5]Is. 44:21-22

[6]Is. 48:8-9

[7]Is. 63:9-10

Spiritum Sanctum. Quos omnes dies saeculi exaltavit quo tempore contumaces fuerunt aut exacerbantes Spiritum Sanctum?

Iterum aperte Deus uni corpori firmitatem et interitum promittit dicens: *Hierusalem civitas dives, tabernacula quae non commovebuntur, neque agitabuntur pali tabernaculi tui in aeternum tempus, neque funes eius rumpentur.* Et adiecit: *Rupti sunt funes tui quia non valuit arbor navis tuae, inclinaverunt vela tua et non tollet signum donec tradatur in perditionem.*

Iterum breviter bipertitum ostenditur Christi corpus: *Fusca sum et decora.* Absit enim ut Ecclesia *quae non habet maculam aut rugam,* quam Dominus suo sanguine sibi mundavit, aliqua ex parte fusca sit nisi in parte sinistra per quam *nomen Dei blasphematur in gentibus.* Alias tota speciosa est, sicut dicit: *Tota speciosa es proxima mea et reprehensio non est in te.* Etenim dicit qua de causa sit fusca et speciosa: *Ut tabernaculum Cedar ut pellis Salomonis.* Duo tabernacula ostendit, regium et seruile: utrumque tamen semen Abrahae; Cedar enim filius est Ismahel. Alio denique loco cum isto Cedar, id est cum seruo ex Abraham, diuturnam mansionem, sic ingemescit Ecclesia dicens: *Heu me quoniam peregrinatio mea longinqua facta est, habitavi cum tabernaculis Cedar, multum peregrinata est anima mea. Cum odientibus pacem eram pacificus, cum loquebar illis debellabant me.* Non possumus autem dicere tabernaculum Cedar praeter Ecclesiam esse. Ipse autem dicit tabernaculum *Cedar et Salomonis* unde *fusca sum* inquit *et decora;* non enim Ecclesia in his qui foris sunt fusca est. Hoc mysterio Dominus in Apocalypsi septem angelos dicit, id est Ecclesiam septiformem, nunc sanctos et praeceptorum custodes, nunc eosdem multorum criminum reos et paenitentia dignos ostendit. Et in Evangelio unum praepositorum corpus diversi meriti manifestat dicens: *Beatus ille servus quem adveniens dominus illius invenerit ita facientem,* et de eodem: *Si autem nequam ille servus,* quem *Dominus dividit in duas partes.* Dico numquid omnem dividet aut findet?

all the days of their life, when were they rebellious or when did they grieve the Holy Spirit?

Again, God plainly promises to the one body both that it will be kept safe and that it will be destroyed when he says, "Jerusalem, a rich city, whose tents will not be moved, nor will the pegs of your tent ever be disturbed or its ropes broken," and then adds, "your lines have been broken because the mast of your ship failed, your sails hung slack, and it will not raise its pennon until it is given over to destruction."[1]

Again, the bipartite character of Christ's body is indicated in brief: "I am black and beautiful."[2] By no means is the church—"which has no spot or wrinkle,"[3] which the Lord cleansed by his own blood—black in any part, except in the left-hand part through which "the name of God is blasphemed among the gentiles."[4] Otherwise it is wholly beautiful, as he says: "you are wholly beautiful, my love, and there is no fault in you."[5] And indeed she says why it is that she is both black and beautiful: "like the tent of Kedar, like the tent-curtain of Solomon."[6] She shows that there are two tents, one royal and one servile. Yet both spring from Abraham, for Kedar is Ishmael's son. And furthermore, in another passage, the church groans that it has dwelt so long with this Kedar, i.e., with the servant descended from Abraham: "Woe is me that my sojourn has been so lengthy, that I have lived among the tents of Kedar. Too long has my soul been on sojourn. With those who hate peace, I was peaceful; when I spoke to them, they made war against me."[7] Yet we cannot claim that the tent of Kedar is outside the church. She herself mentions the "tent of Kedar" and "of Solomon"; and that is why she says, "I am black and beautiful." Those who are outside the church do not make it black. It is in virtue of this mystery that, in the Apocalypse, the Lord now calls the seven angels (i.e.,the septiform church) holy and keepers of his precepts and now shows the same angels to be guilty of many crimes and in need of repentance.[8] And in the gospel he makes it clear that one of the leaders is a body of diverse merits when he says, "blessed is that servant whom his master, when he comes, finds at this work," and then adds, speaking of the same servant, "but if that wicked servant . . . ." This wicked servant "the Lord will split into two parts." I ask, will he split or divide the whole servant? Note then that it is not the

---

[1] Is. 33:20, 23
[2] Song 1:5
[3] Eph. 5:27
[4] Rom. 2:24
[5] Song 4:7
[6] Song 1:5
[7] Ps. 120:5-7
[8] See Rev. 2, 3.

Denique non totum sed *partem eius cum hypocritis ponet,* in uno enim corpus ostendit.

Hoc itaque mysterio accipiendum est per omnes Scripturas sicubi Deus dicit ad merita Israhel periturum aut hereditatem suam execrabilem. Apostolus enim copiose ita disputat, maxime ad Romanos, in parte accipiendum quicquid de toto corpore dictum est. *Ad Israhel* inquit *quid dicit? Tota die expandi manus meas ad plebem contradicentem.* Et ut ostenderet de parte dictum, *Dico,* inquit, *Numquid reppulit Deus hereditatem suam? Absit. Nam et ego Israehelita sum ex semine Abraham tribu Beniamin. Non reppulit Deus plebem suam quam praescivit.* Et post quam docuit quem ad modum haec locutio intellegenda esset, eodem genere locutionis ostendit unum corpus et bonum esse et malum dicens: *Secundum Evangelium quidem inimici propter vos, secundum electionem autem dilecti propter patres.* Numquid idem dilecti qui inimici, aut potest in Caifan utrumque convenire? Ita Dominus in omnibus Scripturis unum corpus seminis Abrahae in omnibus crescere et florere atque perire testatur.

III. De promissis et lege.

Auctoritas est divina neminem aliquando ex operibus legis iustificari potuisse. Eadem auctoritate firmissimum est numquam defuisse qui legem facerent et iustificarentur.

Scriptum est: *Quaecumque lex loquitur his qui in lege sunt dicit, ut omne os obstruatur et subditus fiat omnis mundus Deo, quia non iustificabitur ex lege omnis caro in conspectu eius. Per legem enim cognitio peccati.* Iterum: *Peccatum vestri non dominabitur, non enim estis sub lege.* Iterum: *Et nos in Christum credimus ut iustificemur ex fide et non ex operibus legis, quia non iustificabitur omnis caro ex operibus legis.* Iterum: *Si enim data esset lex quae posset vivificare, omni modo ex lege esset iustitia. Sed conclusit Scriptura omnia sub peccato ut promissio ex fide Iesu Christi daretur credentibus.* Sed dicet quis: a Christo et infra non iustificat lex, suo tamen

whole, but "his part" that "he will put with the hypocrites";[1] for he is showing us the body in one person.

Accordingly it is by this mystery that we must interpret, throughout the scriptures, any passage where God says that Israel will perish as it deserves or that his own inheritance is accursed. For the apostle often argues, especially in Romans, that whatever is said of the whole body must be interpreted as applying to the part. "With respect to Israel, what does he say? All day I reached out my hands to a rebellious people." And to show that this refers to the part, he says, "I ask, has God rejected his inheritance? Not at all. For I am myself an Israelite, descended from Abraham by the tribe of Benjamin. God has not rejected his people whom he foreknew."[2] And after he has taught us how we are to understand this form of expression, he uses the same kind of expression to show that the one body is both good and evil when he says, "as regards the gospel they are enemies for your sake, but as regards election they are loved for their fathers' sake."[3] Are the enemies the same as the ones who are loved? Can both descriptions apply to Caiaphas? Thus, in all the scriptures, the Lord gives testimony that the one body of Abraham's line, in every case, both grows and flourishes and goes to ruin.

III. The Promises and the Law

Divine authority has it that no one can ever be justified by the works of the law. By the same authority it is absolutely certain that there have always been some who do the law and are justified.

It is written: "whatever the law says it says to those who are under the law so as to silence every mouth and to make the whole world subject to God, for no flesh will be justified in his sight by keeping the law. For through the law comes knowledge of sin."[4] Again: "sin will have no dominion over you, for you are not under the law."[5] Again: "we also believe in Christ in order to be justified by faith and not by doing the law, because no flesh will be justified by doing the law."[6] Again: "if the law we were given had been capable of bringing life, righteousness would indeed have come by the law. But scripture included all things under sin so that the promise, which comes by faith in Jesus Christ, might be given to those who believe."[7] But someone is sure to say: now that Christ has come, the law does not justify; but in its own time it did.

---

[1]Mt. 24:46, 48, 51
[2]Rom. 10:21-11:2
[3]Rom. 11:28
[4]Rom. 3:19-20
[5]Rom. 6:14
[6]Gal. 2:16
[7]Gal. 3:21-22

tempore iustificavit. Huic occurrit auctoritas apostoli Petri, qui cum gentes a fratribus sub iugo legis cogerentur sic ait: *Quid temptatis Dominum imponere volentes iugum super collum discentium quod neque patres nostri neque nos potuimus portare.* Et apostolus Paulus: *Cum essemus* inquit *in carne passiones peccatorum quae per legem sunt operabantur in membris nostris ut fructum afferrent morti.*

Et contra idem apostolus dicit: *Iustitia quae ex lege est conversatur sine querella.* Quodsi tanti apostoli auctoritas deesset, quid dici potuit contra testimonium Domini dicentis: *Ecce vere Israhelita in quo dolus non est.* Quod etsi Dominus hoc testimonium non dignaretur perhibere, quis tam sacrilegus, quis tam tumore stuporis elatus diceret Mosen et prophetas vel omnes sanctos legem non fecisse aut iustificatos non esse? Cum et Scriptura dicat de Zacharia et uxore eius: *Erant iusti ambo in conspectu Dei ambulantes in omnibus mandatis et iustificationibus sine querella;* et Dominus non venerit *vocare iustos sed peccatores.*

Lex autem quomodo iustificare potuit a peccato, quae ad hoc data est ut peccatum multiplicaretur? Sicut scriptum est: *Lex autem subintravit ut multiplicaretur peccatum.* Illud autem scire debemus et tenere: numquam omnino interceptum esse semen Abrahae ab Isaac usque in hodiernum diem. Semen autem Abrahae non carnale sed spiritale, quod non ex lege sed ex promissione est. Alterum enim semen carnale est, quod est ex lege *a monte Sina quod est Agar in servitutem generans. Ille quidem qui de ancilla carnaliter natus est, qui autem ex libera ex promissione.* Non esse autem semen Abrahae nisi quod ex fide est apostolus dicit: *Cognoscitis ergo quoniam qui ex fide sunt hi sunt filii Abrahae.* Et iterum: *Vos autem fratres secundum Isaac promissionis filii estis.*

Against this stands the authority of the apostle Peter. When the brethren were compelling the gentiles to accept the yoke of the law, he said: "why are you provoking the Lord with your desire to impose on the disciples a yoke which neither our fathers nor we ourselves were able to bear?"[1] And the apostle Paul says: "while we were in the flesh, the sinful passions, aroused by the law, were at work in our members to bear fruit for death."[2]

On the other hand, the same apostle says: "as to righteousness, which comes from the law, I lived a life without blame."[3] And even if we did not have the authority of such an apostle, what could we say against the testimony of the Lord's own words: "Behold, an Israelite indeed, in whom there is no guile."[4] And even if the Lord had not deigned to provide this testimony, who would be so sacrilegious or so swollen with stupidity as to say either that Moses and the prophets and all the saints did not do the law or that they were not justified? Especially when scripture says of Zechariah and his wife that "they both were righteous in God's sight, walking in all his commandments and ordinances without blame,"[5] and since the Lord comes not "to call the righteous, but sinners."[6]

Yet how could the law justify from sin when the purpose for which it was given was to multiply sin? As it is written, "the law came to multiply sin."[7] Nevertheless we ought to know and to hold fast to this point: the line of Abraham's descent has never been broken from Isaac right down to the present day. And Abraham's line is not carnal but spiritual, because it comes not from the law but from the promise. There is another, carnal line, which does come from the law. "from Mount Sinai, which is Hagar, bearing children for slavery. Indeed the child of the slave was born according to the flesh, but the child of the free woman as the result of the promise."[8] But the apostle says that there is no line of Abraham except the one which is by faith: "so you see that it is those who rely on faith who are the sons of Abraham."[9] And again: "now you, brethren, like Isaac, are sons of the promise."[10]

---

[1]Acts 15:10

[2]Rom. 7:5

[3]Phil. 3:6

[4]Jn. 1:47

[5]Lk. 1:6

[6]Mt. 9:13. Tyconius concludes from this passage that there were righteous as well as sinners.

[7]Rom. 5:20

[8]Gal. 4:24, 23

[9]Gal. 3:7

[10]Gal. 4:28

Semen ergo Abrahae non ex lege sed ex promissione est, quod ex Isaac iugiter mansit. Si autem constat semen Abrahae ante legem fuisse, et illud esse semen Abrahae quod ex fide est, constat et quia numquam fuit ex lege. Non enim potuit et ex lege esse et ex fide. Lex enim et fides diversa res est, quia lex non est fidei sed operum sicut scriptum est: *Lex non est ex fide, sed Qui fecerit ea vivet in eis.* Abraham ergo fide filios semper habuit, lege numquam. *Non enim per legem promissio est Abrahae aut semini eius ut heres esset mundi, sed per iustitiam fidei. Si enim qui per legem ipsi sunt heredes, evacuata est fides, abolita est promissio; lex enim iram operatur.* Si ergo nec fides nec promissio Abrahae destrui ullo modo potest, ab ortu suo iugiter mansit. Nec data lege impedita est quo minus Abrahae filii secundum promissionem fide generarentur. Dicit enim apostolus *post CCCC et XXX annos* datam legem non obfuisse nec destruxisse promissionem. *Si enim ex lege, non iam ex promissione; Abrahae autem per repromissionem donavit Deus.* Et alio loco: *Lex ergo adversus promissa? Absit.* Videmus legem ad promissionem non pertinere nec aliquando alteram in alteram impegisse sed utramque ordinem suum tenuisse. Quia sicut lex numquam fidei obfuit, ita nec fides legem destruxit, sicut scriptum est: *Legem ergo destruimus per fidem? Absit, sed legem statuimus,* id est firmamus, invicem namque firmant.

Ergo filii Abrahae non ex lege sunt, sed ex fide per repromissionem. Quaerendum autem quem ad modum hi qui ex operibus legis negantur potuisse iustificari, in lege positi et legem operantes iustificati fuerint. Quaerendum praeterea cur post promissionem fidei, quae nullo modo destrui potest, data est lex quae non est ex fide, ex cuius operibus nemo iustificaretur quia *quotquot ex operibus legis sunt sub maledicto sunt. Scriptum est enim: Maledictus qui non permanserit in omnibus quae scripta sunt in libro legis ut faciat ea.*

Apostolus denique huic quaestioni prospiciens, cum assereret omni modo fillos Abrahae dono Dei semper fuisse per fidem non per legem

Therefore the line of Abraham, which has remained unbroken from Isaac on, comes not from the law but from the promise. Now if it is true that the line of Abraham existed before the law and that the line of Abraham is the one that comes by faith, then it is also true that it never came by the law. For it could not stem both from the law and from faith. For law and faith are quite different things, since the law is not of faith but of works, as it is written: "the law is not based on faith, but he who does them shall live in them."[1] Therefore Abraham always had sons by faith, never by the law. "For the promise to Abraham and his descendants, that they would inherit the world, comes not through the law, but through the righteousness of faith. For if those who rely on the law are the heirs, faith is pointless and the promise abolished; for the law works wrath."[2] Thus, if neither faith nor the promise to Abraham can in any way be undone, the line has remained unbroken from its origin. Nor did the giving of the law cause any impediment to obstruct the begetting of sons of Abraham by faith according to the promise. For the apostle says that the law, given "four hundred and thirty years later,"[3] did not cancel or undo the promise. "For if by the law, then no longer by promise; but God gave it to Abraham by promise."[4] And in another passage: "is the law, then, against the promises? By no means."[5] So we see that the law does not pertain to the promise, nor has the one ever impinged upon the other. Rather each has held to its own order. For just as the law has never cancelled faith, so neither has faith undone the law, as it is written: "have we then undone the law through faith? Not at all; rather we uphold the law,"[6] i.e., we confirm it, for each confirms the other.

Therefore sons of Abraham do not come from the law, but from faith by the promise. But we still have to ask how those who, it is said, could not be justified by doing the law were justified all the same, even while subject to the law and doing the law. And further, we must ask why, after the promise of faith which can in no way be undone, the law was still given, since the law is not from faith and since no one is justified by doing its works because "everyone who relies on the works of the law is under a curse. For it is written: cursed be everyone who does not persist in observing all that is written in the book of the law."[7]

When the apostle asserted that sons of Abraham by God's gift have always come through faith and not through the law of works, he

---

[1]Gal. 3:12
[2]Rom. 4:13-15
[3]Gal. 3:17
[4]Gal. 3:18
[5]Gal. 3:21
[6]Rom. 3:31
[7]Gal. 3:10

factorum, ex alterius persona respondit sibi dicens: *Quid ergo lex factorum?* Id est, si ex fide filii cur data est lex factorum, cum sufficeret promissio generandis filiis Abrahae et fide nutriendis, *quia Iustus ex fide vivit?* Ante quam enim se interrogasset *Quid ergo lex factorum,* iam dixerat ut viverent qui ex lege iustificari non possent hoc modo: *Quoniam autem ex lege nemo iustificatur apud Deum, iustus autem ex fide vivit.* Ostendit propterea dictum esse per prophetam *ex fide vivit,* ut manifestum fieret quem ad modum viverent qui legem facere non potuissent.

Sed minus liquet quid sit *Iustus ex fide vivit.* Non enim potuit quisquam iustus in lege positus vivere nisi opera legis fecisset et omnia opera; sin minus maledictus esset. Dedit Deus legem: dixit *Non concupisces.* Statim *occasione accepta peccatum per mandatum operatum est omnem concupiscentiam.* Necesse est enim *passiones peccatorum quae per legem* sunt operari *in membris* eius qui in lege est. Propterea enim data est *ut abundaret peccatum,* quia *virtus peccati lex. Venundatus* autem *sub peccato iam non quod vult operatur bonum, sed quod non vult malum, consentit enim legi secundum interiorem hominem.* Expugnatur autem *altera lege* membrorum trahiturque *captivus* neque aliquando liberari potuit nisi sola gratia per fidem.

Est autem crimen magnum perfidiae non adtendisse genus armorum quibus violentia peccati expugnaretur: contra magnificae fidei est inquisisse et vidisse. Est ergo sacrilega mens et male de Deo sentiens quae, cum legem nullo modo humanitus posse fieri et ad ulciscendum paratam videret, non intellexit esse aliquod remedium vitae, nec fieri potuisse ut bonus Deus qui sciebat legem non potuisse fieri alterum vitae aditum non reliquisset, et adversum homines quos ad vitam fecerat undique versum vitae vias clusisset. Hoc fides non tulit, non admisit,

anticipated this question. Adopting the role of an outside questioner, he responded to his own words by asking, "why then the law of works?"[1] That is, if sons come from faith, why was the law of works given, when the promise was sufficient to beget sons of Abraham and to nourish them by faith "since the righteous man has life by faith"?[2] For, before asking himself, "why then the law of works," he had already said that those who cannot be justified by the law do have life: "no one is justified before God by the law, but the righteous man has life by faith."[3] He showed us that the prophet said, "has life by faith,"[4] in order to make it clear how those who could not do the law did have life.

But what is not so clear is what it means to say, "the righteous man has life by faith." For no righteous man, subject to the law, was able to have life unless he had done the works of the law; and that means all the works of the law. Otherwise he was cursed. God gave the law; he said, "you shall not covet." Immediately, "once the opportunity opened, sin produced all kinds of covetousness through the commandment."[5] For "the sinful passions," which are "aroused by the law," are inevitably at work "in the members" of anyone who is subject to the law.[6] For the law was given precisely "that sin might abound,"[7] since "the power of sin is the law."[8] "Sold under sin, he no longer does the good he wants, but the evil he does not want, for inwardly he gives his consent to the law."[9] He is vanquished by the "other law" in his members, is taken "captive," and can only be set free by grace through faith.[10]

But it is a matter of great and criminal faithlessness not to have paid attention to the kind of weapons by which the violence of sin is overcome. To have asked and to have seen, on the other hand, belong to the glory of faith. Therefore it is only the sacrilegious mind, one that thinks ill of God, that did not understand—when it saw that it was not humanly possible to do the law and that the law was designed to punish—that there was still a remedy of life and that the good God (who knew that no one could do the law) could not possibly have left no other way of gaining life or have closed all the paths of life against men (whom he had made for life). Faith did not tolerate this, did not accept

---

[1]Gal. 3:19

[2]Gal. 3:11

[3]Gal. 3:11

[4]Hab. 2:4

[5]Rom. 7:7-8

[6]Rom. 7:5

[7]Rom 5:20

[8]1 Cor. 15:56

[9]Rom. 7:14, 15, 16, 22

[10]Rom. 7:23, 24, 25

sed cum infirmitate carnis et virtute peccati urgueretur dedit Deo claritatem. Sciens Dominum bonum et iustum et viscera miserationis suae contra opera manuum suarum non clusisse, intellexit esse iter ad vitam et faciendae legis remedium vidit. Deus enim cum diceret *Non concupisces* non nudavit quem ad modum id provenire posset, sed severe atque decise dixit *Non concupisces:* quoniam id fide repperiendum reliquit. Si enim mandaret a se proventum postulari, et legem destruxerat et fidem. Ut quid enim legem daret, si legem in omnibus facturum polliceretur? Aut quid fidei relinqueret, si fidem auxilium pollicendo praeveniret? Nunc autem bono fidei dedit legem ministram mortis, ut amatores vitae fide vitam viderent, et iusti fide viverent qui opus legis non ex sua virtute sed ex Dei dono fieri posse crederent. Lex enim a carne fieri non potest; quaecumque facta non fuerit punit.

Quae ergo spes homini faciendae legis et fugiendae mortis nisi opis et misericordiae Dei, quam fides invenit? *Caro legi Dei subiecta non est, neque enim potest. Qui autem in carne sunt Deo placere non possunt. Vos autem non estis in carne sed in spiritu, si quidem Spiritus Dei in vobis est. Si quis autem Spiritum Christi non habet, hic non est eius.* Ostendit Spiritum Dei et Christi idem esse. Ostendit praeterea qui Spiritum Dei habuerit in carne non esse. Si ergo unus est Spiritus Dei et Christi, prophetae et sancti qui Spiritum Dei habuerunt Spiritum Christi habuerunt. Si Spiritum Dei habuerunt, in carne non fuerunt; si in carne non fuerunt, legem fecerunt: quia caro est inimica in Deum et *legi* eius *subiecta non est*; qui ergo ad Deum confugit accepit Spiritum Dei, quo accepto mortificata est caro; qua mortificata potuit facere legem spiritalis, liberatus a lege: *quia*

it. Rather, when pressed by the weakness of the flesh and the power of sin, it gave the glory to God. Knowing that the Lord is good and just and that he had not closed the bowels of his mercy against the works of his own hands, it understood that there is a road to life and saw the remedy for doing the law. For when God said, "you shall not covet," he did not lay bare how that could happen but simply said, austerely and concisely, "you shall not covet." He left it to faith to discover the means. For if he had commanded that we ask him for the means, he would have undone both the law and faith. What would be the point of giving the law, if he were to promise beforehand that he would do the law in everyone? And what would he leave to faith if he were to forestall faith by promising his aid?[1] As it is, however, he has given the law as a minister of death for faith's benefit, so that those who love life might see life by faith and the righteous might have life by faith, believing that the work of the law cannot be done by their own power but only by God's gift. For the law cannot be done by the flesh; and whatever is not done it punishes.

What hope, then, does man have of doing the law and escaping death? Only the hope of God's help and mercy which faith brings. "The flesh does not submit to God's law, for it cannot; and those who are in the flesh cannot please God. But you are not in the flesh, you are in the Spirit, if in fact the Spirit of God is in you. But anyone who does not have the Spirit of Christ does not belong to him."[2] Here he shows us that the Spirit of God and the Spirit of Christ are one and the same. Beyond this, he shows that the person who has the Spirit of God is not in the flesh. If therefore the Spirit of God and the Spirit of Christ are one, the prophets and saints who had the Spirit of God had the Spirit of Christ. If they had the Spirit of God, they were not in the flesh. If they were not in the flesh, they did the law. For it is the flesh that is hostile to God and "does not submit to his law." Therefore anyone who fled to God for refuge received the Spirit of God. And when the Spirit of God was received, the flesh was mortified. When the flesh was mortified, the spiritual man was able to

---

[1] Tyconius' point is that, if God had, in giving the law, *explicitly* directed us to seek divine aid in doing the law, both the purpose of the law and the place of faith would have been undermined. The purpose of the law was to drive persons to faith; and the place of faith was to sustain the confidence that God would not allow human beings to perish under the burden of the law, but would supply divine aid, i.e., the gift of the Spirit who enacts the law in the person of the believer and thus enables the believer to fulfill the law. Subsequent to Christ's coming, of course, the promise of divine aid is explicit. Thus the difference between the period prior to Christ and the period subsequent to Christ is not a difference in the interaction between the law, faith and grace, but simply the difference between unrevealed and revealed grace (see p. 31). That is why Tyconius will argue (p. 33) that the righteous in Israel were called from faith to the *same* faith and that the difference between the Spirit, faith and grace prior to Christ and subsequent to Christ is a difference in measure, but not in kind.

[2] Rom. 8:7-9

iusto non est lex posita; et iterum: *Si Spiritu* Dei *agimini non estis sub lege.*

Qua re manifestum est quia patres nostri qui Spiritum Dei habuerunt non fuerunt sub lege. Quamdiu enim quis in carne est, id est Spiritum Dei non habet, dominatur eius lex. Si autem tradiderit se gratiae, moritur legi et facit in illo legem Spiritus, mortua carne quae legi Dei subiecta esse non potest. Quod enim gerebatur id etiam nunc geritur. Non enim quia sub lege non sumus cessavit interdictio illa concupiscentiae et non magis aucta est; sed nos in revelatam gratiam concurrimus per fidem, edocti a Domino opus legis de eius misericordia postulare et dicere: *Fiat voluntas tua,* et *Libera nos a malo;* illi autem in non revelatam per eandem fidem coacti metu mortis, quam ministra lege parato gladio intentari videbant.

Lex data est *donec veniret semen cui promissum est* et evangelizaret fidem. Antea vero lex cogebat in fidem, quia sine lege non possit exprimi fides ad exquirendam Dei gratiam, eo quod peccatum virtutem non haberet. Data vero lege *passiones quae per legem sunt operabantur in membris nostris* urguentes in peccatum, ut vel necessitate urgueremur in fidem quae imploraret gratiam Dei in auxilium tolerantiae. Custodiam carceris passi sumus, legem minantem mortem et undique versum insuperabili muro ambientem, cuius ambitus sola una ianua fuit gratia. Huic ianuae custos fides praesidebat, ut nemo illum carcerem effugeret, nisi cui fides aperuisset; qui hanc ianuam non pulsaret intra septum legis moreretur. Legem paedagogum passi sumus, qui nos cogeret studere fidei, qui nos cogeret in Christum. Dicit enim apostolus propterea datam legem, ut nos custodia sui concluderet in fidem, quam futurum erat revelari in Christum qui est *finis legis*, quo vixerunt omnes qui fide gratiam Dei exquisierunt. *Prius* inquit *quam veniret fides, sub lege*

do the law, having been set free from the law since "the law is not laid down for the just"[1] and again, "if you are led by the Spirit" of God "you are not subject to the law."[2]

In this light, it is manifest that our fathers, who had the Spirit of God, were not subject to the law. So long as a person is in the flesh, i.e., does not have the Spirit of God, he is under the law's dominion. But if he gives himself to grace, he dies to the law; and the Spirit does the law in him, since the flesh which cannot submit to God's law is dead. And what held true before still holds true now. The fact that we are not under the law does not mean that the ban against coveting has come to an end; rather it has even more force. But we, through faith, take refuge in revealed grace, taught by the Lord to ask for his mercy in order to do the law and to say, "your will be done," and "deliver us from evil,"[3] while they, through the same faith, took refuge in unrevealed grace, compelled by fear of death which they saw stretched out against them with the law as its minister, its sword at the ready.

The law was given "until the offspring to whom the promise was made should come"[4] and should preach faith. Until then, it was the law that compelled to faith because, without the law, sin would have lacked its power[5] and faith, as a consequence, could not have been pressed into seeking God's grace. But once the law was given, "the passions, aroused by the law, were at work in our members,"[6] driving us into sin so that, by necessity as it were, we might be driven to faith which implores God's grace to help us endure. We were shut up in prison, with the law threatening death and enclosing us on all sides with an insurmountable wall. The only gate in the enclosure was grace, and at this gate faith stood guard so that no one could escape the prison unless faith had opened the gate for him. Anyone who did not knock at this gate remained within the law's enclosing wall. We endured the law as our guardian, compelling us to strive for faith, compelling us to Christ. For the apostle says that the law was given precisely to hold us under its custody for the sake of faith, which was to be revealed in Christ who is "the end of the law"[7] and by whom all those who sought God's grace by faith gained life. "Before faith came," he says, "we were kept under the custody of the law,

---

[1] 1 Tim. 1:9
[2] Gal. 5:18
[3] Mt. 6:10, 13
[4] Gal. 3:19
[5] An allusion to 1 Cor. 15:56.
[6] Rom. 7:5
[7] Rom. 10:4

*custodiebamur conclusi in eam fidem quam futurum erat revelari.   Lex
itaque paedagogus noster fuit in Christo, ut ex fide iustificaremur.*

Lex inquam fidei erat demonstratrix.   Sed dicit quis: si in utilitate
fidei data est lex, cur non ab origine seminis Abrahae, si quidem iuge
fuit?   Re vera iuge fuit: iugis et fides ut genitrix filiorum Abrahae, iugis et
lex per dinoscentiam boni et mali.   Sed post promissionem filiorum
Abrahae, multiplicatis eis secundum carnem, multiplicandum erat et
semen Abrahae quod non est nisi ex fide.   Quae multiplicatio evenire non
posset sine adiutorio legis multiplicatae, ut multitudo in fidem necdum
revelatam ut iam dictum est vel necessitate deduceretur.   Providentia
itaque Dei factum est augendo gubernandoque semini Abrahae, ut
severitate et metu legis multi compellerentur in fidem, et semen
fulciretur usque ad fidei revelationem.   *Lex autem subintroivit ut
multiplicaretur peccatum.   Ubi* inquit *multiplicatum est peccatum supe-
abundavit gratia.*   Non dixit *data est* sed *superabundavit.*   Ab initio enim
data est per Christum fugientibus legis molestias atque dominium.
Abundavit autem multiplicata lege, superabundavit uero in omnem
carnem revelata in Christum, qui veniens *restaurare quae in caelo et quae
in terra evangelizavit fidem his qui proxime et qui longe,* id est peccatoribus
Israhel et gentibus.

Iusti enim Israhel ex fide in eandem fidem vocati sunt.   Idem
namque Spiritus, eadem fides, eadem gratia per Christum semper data
est, quorum plenitudinem veniens remoto legis velamine omni genti
largitus est, quae modo non genere a futuris differebant.   Aliter enim
numquam fuit semen Abrahae.

Quod si quisquam praeter haec iustificatus est, filius Abrahae non
fuit.   Quoniam filius Abrahae dici non potest, si ex lege et non sicut
Abraham ex fide iustificatus est.   Ab eadem namque imagine gratiae et
spiritus in eandem transisse Ecclesiam docet apostolus dicens: *Nos autem*

held in confinement for the faith which was to be revealed. Thus the law was our guardian in Christ, that we might be justified by faith."[1]

The law, I say, was what showed us faith. But someone asks: if the law was given as an aid to faith, why was it not given from the beginning of Abraham's line if that line was indeed uninterrupted? Most certainly it was uninterrupted. Uninterrupted, too, was faith as the begetter of Abraham's sons; and also uninterrupted was the law, through the knowledge of good and evil.[2] But after the promise of sons to Abraham, when his line had been multiplied according to the flesh, the offspring of Abraham who came only by faith had also to be multiplied. But this increase could not take place without the help of an increase in the law so that a multitude might be led, by necessity as it were (as I have already said), to faith as yet unrevealed. By God's providence, then, this took place for the increase and for the guidance of Abraham's line, so that many might be compelled to faith by fear of the law's severity and the line be kept strong until faith was revealed. "The law came to multiply sin. Where sin was multiplied," he said, "grace abounded all the more."[3] He did not say grace "was given," but grace "abounded all the more." For it was given from the beginning, through Christ, to those who sought escape from the law's vexing dominion. It abounded, however, when the law had been increased; and it abounded all the more when it was revealed to all flesh in Christ who came "to restore things in heaven and things on earth"[4] and "preached" faith "to those who were near and those who were far off,"[5] i.e., to sinners in Israel and to the gentiles.[6]

For the righteous in Israel were simply called from faith to the same faith. For the same Spirit, the same faith, the same grace was always given through Christ. When the veil of the law had been removed, he came and bestowed the fullness of these on all people. But what was given before differed only in measure, not in kind, from what was to come. Otherwise there never was a line of Abraham.

But if anyone was justified apart from these, he was no son of Abraham. No one can be called a son of Abraham, if he was justified by the law and not, like Abraham, by faith. For the apostle teaches us that the church passed from the one image of grace and the Spirit into the

---

[1]Gal. 3:23-24

[2]Tyconius counts the knowledge of good and evil as a version of the law present before the law was given in written form at Sinai.

[3]Rom. 5:20

[4]Eph. 1:10

[5]Eph. 2:17

[6]But not, it should be noted, to the righteous in Israel. The righteous in Israel are the ones who are called from faith to the same faith, for they had already been driven to faith by the law before Christ came to preach faith.

omnes revelata facie gloriam Dei speculantes in eandem imaginem commutamur a claritate in claritatem. Dicit et ante passionem Domini gloriam fuisse et negat ex lege excludi, id est exprimi, produci, effici, potuisse. Unde manifestum est ex fide fuisse. *Ubi ergo* inquit *gloriatio? Exclusa est. Per quam legem? Numquid operum? Non: sed per legem fidei. Quid enim Scriptura dicit? Credidit Abraham Deo et deputatum est ei ad iustitiam.* In gloriam ex eadem *gloria* transivimus quae non fuit ex lege.

Si enim ex operibus, fuit gloria, *sed non ad Deum.* Etenim impossibile est sine gratia Dei habere aliquem gloriam. Una est enim gloria et uno genere semper fuit. Nemo enim vicit nisi cui Deus vicerit, quod non est in lege sed qui fecerit; in fide autem infirmum facit Deus adversarium nostrum, propterea *ut qui gloriatur in Domino glorietur.* Si enim quod vincimus nostrum non est, non est ex operibus sed ex fide, et nihil est quod ex nobis gloriemur. Nihil enim habemus quod non accepimus. Si sumus, ex Deo sumus, ut magnitudo virtutis sit Dei et non ex nobis. Omne opus nostrum fides est, quae quanta fuerit tantum Deus operatur nobiscum. In hoc gloriatur Salomon, scisse se non ex homine sed ex Dei dono esse continentiam. *Cum scivi* inquit *quoniam aliter non possum esse continens nisi Deus dederit, et hoc ipsum autem erat sapientiae, scire cuius esset hoc donum, adii Dominum et deprecatus sum.* Iudicio Salomonis credendum est non ex operibus sed gratia Dei omnes iustificatos, qui scierunt opus legis a Deo impetrandum quo possent gloriari.

Dicit autem apostolus quem ad modum *omnis caro non glorietur in conspectu Dei:* mali omni modo quod Deum non cognoverint, iusti quod non suum sed opus Dei sint. *Inutilia* inquit *et abiecta elegit Deus, quae non sunt ut quae sunt evacuaret, ut non gloriatur omnis caro in conspectu Dei. Ex ipso autem vos estis in Christo Iesu, qui factus est nobis sapientia a Deo et*

same image, when he says: "and we all, reflecting God's glory with unveiled faces, are being changed into the same image, going from glory to glory."[1] He is saying that there was also a glory before the Lord suffered; and he denies that it could have been forced out—i.e., expressed, produced, brought forth—by the law. Manifestly, then, it came from faith. "What then," he says "of our glorying? It has been forced out. By what law? By the law of works? No. Rather by the law of faith."[2] "For what does scripture say? Abraham believed God, and it was reckoned to him as righteousness."[3] We have passed "to glory" from the same "glory," which did not come from the law.

"For if" it was "from works," there was glory, "but not unto God."[4] Indeed it is impossible for anyone to have glory without God's grace. For there is one glory, and it was always one in kind. For no one has conquered unless God conquered for him; and this belongs not to the law, but to the one who made it. In faith, moreover, God makes our adversary weak precisely so that "he who seeks glory may seek the Lord's glory."[5] For if our victory is not our own doing, it is not the result of works, but of faith; and there is nothing to which we can look for a glory of our own. For we have nothing that we have not received.[6] If we have existence, we have it from God, so that the greatness of this power belongs to God and does not come from ourselves. All our work is faith; and to the extent that we have faith, to that extent God works in us. Solomon finds his glory in this, that he knew his continence did not come from human effort but by God's gift. "Since I knew," he says, "that I could only be continent by God's gift—and this was itself a mark of wisdom, to know to whom this gift belonged—I approached the Lord and entreated him."[7] In the light of Solomon's view, we must believe that it is not by works but by God's grace that all those were justified who knew that doing the law—whereby they could find glory—must be obtained from God.

Moreover the apostle explains how it is that "no flesh may claim glory in God's sight": the evil certainly may not because they do not know God; and the just may not because they are not their own work but God's. "God," he says, "chose what is useless and despised, things that are not, so as to bring to nothing things that are, so that no flesh may claim glory in God's sight. It is his doing that you are in Christ Jesus

---

[1]2 Cor. 3:18

[2]Rom. 3:27. I have used "forced out" to translate *exclusa est* in order to retain something of the obvious and familiar sense ("excluded") while still honoring the meaning that Tyconius gives the term: "produced" or "brought forth."

[3]Rom. 4:3

[4]Rom. 4:2

[5]1 Cor. 1:31

[6]The allusion is to 1 Cor. 4:7.

[7]Wisd. 8:21

iustitia et sanctimonia et redemptio, ut secundum quod scriptum est: qui gloriatur in Domino glorietur. Et iterum: *Gratia estis salvati per fidem. Et hoc non ex vobis, Dei donum est; non ex operibus ne forte quis glorietur. Ipsius enim sumus figmentum creati in Christo.* Sic nulla caro aliquando ex lege, id est ex operibus, iustificari potest, ut omnis iustus ex Deo gloriam haberet.

Est aliud quo nemo glorietur in conspectu Dei. Deus enim sic suis operatur ut sit quod et dimittat, *nemo* est *enim mundus a sorde nec si unius diei sit vita eius.* Et David dicit: *Non introeas in iudicio cum servo tuo, quoniam non iustificabitur coram te omnis vivens.* Et Salomon in prece dedicationis templi: *Non est* inquit *homo qui non peccavit.* Iterum: *Tibi soli deliqui,* et: *Quis enim gloriabitur castum se habere cor, aut quis gloriabitur mundum se esse a peccato?* Parum fuit de casto corde, id est a cogitationibus, nisi et a peccato mundum se nemo gloriaretur. Omnis victoria non ex operibus sed Dei miseratione conceditur, sicut scriptum est: *Qui coronat te in misericordia et miseratione.* Et mater martyrum filio suo sic dicit: *Ut in illa miseratione cum fratribus te recipiam.* Iusti autem perfecerunt voluntatem Dei voto atque conatu quo nituntur et concupiscunt Deo servire.

Non est bene et melius in lege, quae si iustificasset omnes iusti unius essent meriti, quia parem de omnibus exigit observationem; sin minus operaretur maledictio. Sin autem disparis erant meriti—quis quantum credidit sibi dari tantum gratiae Dei miserantis accepit—ergo transformati *a gloria in gloriam sicut a Domini Spiritu,* id est ex eodem in eundem. Tale est enim quia post Christum fides data est quale quia et Spiritus Sanctus, cum semper omnes prophetae et iusti eodem Spiritu vixerint. Non enim aliter vivere potuerunt quam Spiritu fidei. Quotquot

whom God made our wisdom and our righteousness and our holiness and our redemption so that, as it is written, he who seeks glory may seek the Lord's glory."[1]   And again, "by grace you were saved through faith. And this is not your doing; it is God's gift, not the result of works, lest anyone claim a glory of his own.   For we are his handiwork, created in Christ."[2]   Thus no flesh can ever be justified by the law, i.e., by works; and so all the just have their glory from God.

There is another reason why no one may claim glory in God's sight. For God works in those who are his in such a way that there remains something for him to forgive, "for no one" is "without stain, not even if he lives only for one day."[3]   And David says, "Do not enter into judgment with your servant, for no one living will be justified before you."[4]   And in his prayer of dedication for the temple, Solomon says, "there is no one who has not sinned."[5]   Again: "against you only have I done wrong,"[6] and: "who will claim the glory of having a pure heart, or who will claim the glory of being free from sin?"[7]   It was no great thing that no one should claim the glory of a pure heart, i.e., free from scheming, unless it was also true that no one should claim to be free from sin.   No victory comes from works; rather it is granted by God's mercy, as it is written: "who crowns you with tenderness and mercy."[8]   And the martyrs' mother said this to her son: "so that in his mercy I may receive you back again with your brother."[9]   However the just did accomplish God's will in the desire and the striving with which they tried and longed to serve God.

There is no good and better in the law.   If it had justified, all the just would have had exactly the same merit.   For the law demands equal observance from all.   Anything less brings the curse into effect.   But if they were of unequal merit—each received so much of God's grace and mercy as he believed he was given—then they were transformed "from glory to glory, just as from the Spirit of the Lord,"[10] i.e., from the one [Spirit] to the same [Spirit].   For just as faith was given after Christ, so was the Holy Spirit, even though all the prophets and the righteous always lived by the same Spirit.   For there was no other way that they

---

[1]1 Cor. 1:28-31
[2]Eph. 2:8-10
[3]Job 14:4-5 (cf. Septuagint)
[4]Ps. 143:2
[5]1 Kings 8:46
[6]Ps. 51:4
[7]Prov. 20:9
[8]Ps. 103:4
[9]2 Macc. 7:29
[10]2 Cor. 3:18

enim sub lege fuerunt occisi sunt, quia *littera occidit Spiritus autem vivificat*. Et tamen dicit Dominus de eodem Spiritu: *Nisi ego abiero ille non veniet*, cum et apostolis iam dedisset eundem Spiritum. Apostolus autem sic dicit eundem Spiritum apud antiquos fuisse: *Habentes autem eundem Spiritum fidei, sicut scriptum est: credidi propter quod locutus sum*. Eundem Spiritum fidei dixit habuisse eundem qui dixit: *credidi propter quod locutus sum*, et id confirmat dicens: *Et nos credimus ideoque et loquimur*. Dicendo *et nos* ostendit et illos eodem Spiritu fidei credidisse. Unde manifestum est quia haec iusti non ex lege sed Spiritu fidei semper habuerunt.

Et quicquid per Dominum venit plenitudo est, cuius pars fuit per eundem, sicut parvulus qui, cum nihil minus habeat a viro, tamen vir non est, et per incrementa non novorum sed eorundem membrorum in eum venit plenitudo corporis, ut sit perfectus idem tamen qui fuerat parvulus. Re vera *non erat Spiritus Sanctus* ante passionem Domini, sed in illis qui per ipsum praesentem credebant, ut in ipso victore et cuncta perficiente *signati* perficerentur. Nam iusti quos his invenit habuerunt Spiritum Sanctum, ut Symeon et Nathanael Zacharias et Helisabeth et Anna vidua filia Fanuhel.

Promissio ergo a lege separata est, neque cum sit diversum misceri potest, nam conditio infirmat promissionem. Cogimur autem nos loqui ea quae sine igne doloris audire non possumus. Dicunt enim quidam, qui promissionum firmitatem et quae ex lege est transgressionem nesciunt, promisisse quidem Deum Abrahae omnes gentes, sed salvo libero arbitrio, si legem custodissent. Et si pericula imperitiae quorundam in eorum salutem patefacere prodest, sed cum de Deo omnipotente sermo est moderari dicenda debemus, ne silenda refutando memoremus, et ex ore nostro aliena licet audiantur. Quare cum tremore loquentes sua cuique pericula consideranda reliquimus.

could have had life than by the Spirit of faith. For all who were under the law were killed, since "the letter kills, but the Spirit gives life."[1] And yet the Lord says concerning the same Spirit, "unless I go, he will not come,"[2] even though he had already given the same Spirit to the apostles. The apostle, too, says that the same Spirit was with the ancients: "but since we have the same Spirit of faith, as it is written: I believed and therefore I spoke."[3] He stated that the one who said, "I believed and therefore I spoke," had "the same Spirit of faith"; and he confirms this when he says, "we too believe and therefore we too speak."[4] By saying "we too," he shows that the ancients also believed by the same Spirit of faith. So it is manifest that the righteous always had these, not from the law, but by the Spirit of faith.

And whatever the Lord brought is the fullness of which a part was already present through the same Lord. It is like a boy who, although he lacks nothing that a man has, still is not a man. The fullness of his body comes through the growth not of new members but of the same members, so that the boy and the grown man are still one and the same. In truth, "the Holy Spirit had not been given"[5] before the Lord's passion, save to those who believed through the Spirit's presence so that, sealed in him as victor and as the one who brings all things to full perfection, they might themselves be brought to perfection. For the righteous whom the Lord found here did have the Holy Spirit: Simeon, for example, and Nathaniel and Zechariah and Elizabeth and the widow Anna, Phanuel's daughter.

Therefore the promise is distinct from the law; and since they are different, they cannot be mixed. For to add a condition is to weaken the promise. Yet we are forced to say things which we cannot hear without a burning sorrow: for there are some who know neither the firmness of the promises nor the transgression that stems from the law, and they, because they want to preserve free will, claim that God did indeed promise all the nations to Abraham but only if the nations were to keep the law. Even if it is useful to expose the dangers of their ignorance as an aid to their salvation, still—when speaking of the omnipotent God— we have an obligation to tone down the things that need to be said. We do not want to mention, in refuting it, what ought to be left in silence; nor do we want to have alien doctrines heard from our lips. Consequently it is with apprehension that we speak; and we leave each person to consider the dangers in his own case.

---

[1] 2 Cor. 3:6
[2] Jn. 16:7
[3] 2 Cor. 4:13
[4] 2 Cor. 4:13
[5] Jn. 7:39

Manifestum est praescisse Deum futuros de libero arbitrio quos Abrahae promisit aut non futuros. Alterum est duorum: si futuros finita quaestio est, si non futuros fidelis Deus non promitteret. Aut si hoc est statutum apud Deum tunc promissos dare si promissi velint, profecto diceret, ne servus eius *credens quia quod promisit* Deus *potens est et facere* ludificaretur Abraham. Promissio autem illa est quae nihil conditionis incurrit, sin minus nec promissio est firma nec fides integra. Quid enim stabile remanebit in Dei promissione aut in Abrahae fide, si id quod promissum et creditum est in eorum qui promissi sunt penderet arbitrio? Ergo et Deus alienum promisit et Abraham incaute credidit. Ut quid etiam ipsa promissio debitum post modum facta est dicente Deo: *Benedicentur in te omnes gentes terrae, pro eo quod audisti vocem meam et non pepercisti filio tuo dilecto propter me?* Quia autem ex his quibusdam facile est et adversum Abrahae meritum liberi arbitrii calumnia strepere, etiam post mortem ipsius Abrahae debitorem se eius confirmat Deus, et propter eum se statuturum quod eius filio promittebat dicens: *Ero tecum et benedicam te: tibi enim et semini tuo dabo terram hanc; et statuam iurationem meam quam iuravi Abrahae patri tuo, et multiplicabo semen tuum sicut stellas caeli, et dabo tibi et semini tuo omnes gentes terrae, pro eo quod audivit Abraham pater tuus vocem meam.* Ecce firmatum est debitum Abrahae, non enim potuit per liberum arbitrium post mortem amittere quod vivus meruerat.

Noluerunt autem gentes credere. Quid faciet Abraham cui debetur? Quomodo accipiet fidei et temptationis suae debitum, cuius debitore Deo securus fuit? Cui si dictum esset Dabo quod promisi et reddam quod iuravi si voluerint gentes, non crederet sed expectaret fortuitum. Si conditione opus est cum operario esse potest non cum mercede. Operarius enim potest velle accipere aut nolle, non merces reddi aut non reddi.

Clearly God foreknew that the peoples whom he promised to Abraham would come by free will or that they would not. It is one of the two: if that they would, the question is settled; if that they would not, a trustworthy God would have made no promise. Or if we are to suppose of God that he would give the promised peoples only if they themselves should wish to be given, surely he would have said so, lest anyone make sport of his servant Abraham for "believing that God was able to do what he had promised."[1] A true promise has no condition attached; otherwise the promise is not firm, nor does one believe in it without reservation. For what is there to count on either in God's promise or in Abraham's belief, if what was promised and believed depends on the choice of the ones who were promised? It would follow that God promised something beyond his own control and that Abraham was foolish to believe. Then again, why was the promise itself later turned into a debt owed, when God said, "all the nations of the earth will be blessed in you, because you obeyed my voice and, for my sake, did not spare your beloved son?"[2] Moreover, because some find it easy to use this passage to raise doubts even about Abraham's merit, on the pretext of defending free will, God also confirms, after Abraham's death, that he is in debt to him. He states that, on Abraham's account, he will establish what he promised to Abraham's son: "I will be with you and will bless you; for to you and to your descendants I will give this land, and I will fulfill my oath which I swore to Abraham your father. I will multiply your descendants as the stars of heaven, and will give to you and to your descendants all the nations of the earth, because Abraham your father obeyed my voice."[3] Note how the debt to Abraham was confirmed; after his death he could no longer lose through free will what he had earned while alive.[4]

The nations, however, did not want to believe. What will Abraham do? The debt is owed to him. How will he get what is owed to him for his faith and his temptation? He was untroubled about the debt because God was the debtor. If God had said, I will give what I promised and pay what I swore if the nations are willing, Abraham would not have believed but would have awaited what chance might bring. If there must be a condition, it can have to do with the worker but not with the reward. The worker can wish or not wish to receive his reward; but the

---

[1]Rom. 4:21

[2]Gen. 22:18, 16

[3]Gen. 26:3-5

[4]Tyconius' concern, it seems, is to answer the possible objection that the promise to Abraham was conditional not only in the sense that it depended on the will of the people promised to Abraham, but also on Abraham's own will since, in his freedom, he might subsequently act in such a way as to lose the promise. The reiteration of the promise after Abraham's death removes this objection and shows that God treats the promise as a debt that he owes to Abraham, not as a conditional arrangement the outcome of which is uncertain.

Omnes enim gentes in mercedem fidei datae sunt Abrahae sicut Deus dicit: *Merces tua multa est.* Non enim si futuri essent et non quia futuri erant promisit. Quia non propter fidem Abrahae placuit Deo salvas fore omnes gentes, quas non ante fidem Abrahae sed ante mundi constitutionem possedit. Sed quaesivit fidelem cui id donaret ex quo esset quod futurum statuerat. Abraham ergo non id meruit ut essent sed ut per ipsum essent qui futuri erant quos Deus elegerat, et *conformes imaginis filii sui* futuros esse praeviderat. In Genesi namque de praescientia Dei omnes gentes Abrahae promissas Scriptura testatur dicens: *Abraham autem fiens fiet et erit in gentem magnam et multam, et benedicentur in eo omnes gentes terrae. Sciebat enim quia disponebat Abraham filiis suis et domui suae post se, et custodient vias Domini facere iustitiam et iudicium, ut superducat Deus in Abraham quaecumque locutus est ad eum.*

Invenimus autem et conditiones ut: *Si me audieritis et volueritis.* Ubi praescientia Dei, ubi firmitas promissionis in huiusmodi conditionibus? Dicit etiam apostolus propterea ex fide et non ex lege datam esse promissionem ut firma esset promissio. *Lex* inquit *iram operatur; ubi enim non est lex neque transgressio est. Propterea ex fidei ut secundum gratiam firma esset promissio omni semini.* Recte *ut firma esset promissio,* adiecta enim conditione non est firma. Satis enim stultum est et protervum credere in totum corpus convenire quod bipertito corpori dicitur. Absit ut his dicat Deus *si me audieritis* quos sciebat audituros, et quos antequam faceret noverat in imagine Dei perseveraturos, quos et

reward cannot wish to be paid or not to be paid. Now all the nations were given to Abraham in reward for his faith, as God says, "your reward will be very great."[1] For God did not make the promise because the nations might come, but because they would come. It was not on the grounds of Abraham's faith that it pleased God to save all the nations; he already possessed all the nations not simply before Abraham believed but before the very foundation of the world. Rather he sought a man of faith to whom he might give the gift that through him should take place what he had already determined would take place. Thus what Abraham earned by his merit was not that those who were to come—those whom God had chosen and of whom he had foreseen that they would be "conformed to the image of his son"[2]—should actually come, but that they should come through him. For, in Genesis, scripture bears witness that all the nations were promised to Abraham on the basis of God's foreknowledge when it says, "Abraham will surely become and be a great and numerous nation, and all the nations of the earth will be blessed in him. For he knew that Abraham was charging his sons and his household after him, and that they would keep the ways of the Lord, to do righteousness and justice, and so God will bring to Abraham all that he declared to him."[3]

However we do also find conditional statements such as, "if you obey me and are willing."[4] Where is God's foreknowledge, where is the firmness of the promise in conditions of this sort? The apostle, too, says that the promise was given on the basis of faith, and not on the basis of the law, precisely so that the promise would be firm. "The law," he says, "works wrath: for where there is no law, there is no transgression. That is why it rests on faith, so that, in grace, the promise might be firm to all his descendants."[5] He is right to say, "so that the promise might be firm"; for a promise is not firm when a condition is attached. Certainly it is foolish and perverse to believe that something said to the bipartite body pertains to the whole body.[6] God would hardly say, "if you obey me," to those of whom he already knew that they would obey, of whom he knew—even before he made them—that they would persevere in the image of God, the ones whom he promised. The

---

[1]Gen. 15:1

[2]Rom. 8:29

[3]Gen. 18:18-19

[4]Is. 1:19

[5]Rom. 4:15-17

[6]This notion is basic to Tyconius' interpretation of the conditional promises he finds in scripture: they are addressed—and therefore apply—only to a part (the left-hand part) and not to the whole of Christ's body. The left-hand part consists of those whose future faith is not foreknown by God and thus genuinely remains in doubt.

promisit. Non est data conditio, id est lex, nisi impiis et peccatoribus, ut aut ad gratiam confugiant aut iustius puniantur si irritam fecerint.

Ut quid lex ad iustos quibus *lex posita non est,* qui propitio Deo legem sine lege faciunt, qui liberi Deo serviunt, qui ad imaginem et similitudinem Dei et Christi vivunt? Volentes boni sunt. Qui enim sub lege est metu mortis non est apertus homicida; non est talis misericors, non est imago Dei. Displicet illi lex sed metuet ultricem, nec perficere potest, quod non voto sed necessitate faciendum putat. Tradatur necesse est propriae voluntati, ut voluntatis profecto praemium recipiat qui animam non miscuit voluntati Dei. Displicet illi quod Deus voluit. Etenim voluntate malus est qui necessitate bonus est. Lex operi impedimento est non voluntati. Non est coniunctus Deo qui si mali poena non esset malum sequeretur; nec uoluntatem Dei facit qui gemit quod non suam faciat. Et non est misericors qui timet esse crudelis: sub lege est, servus est. Non furtum odit sed poenam metuit. Furetur autem necesse est persuasus et victus, quia carnalis est sub virtute peccati, Spiritum Dei non habens. Qui autem amat bonum imago Dei est et fide dominica vivit, ut heres iam non sit ancillae filius qui accipit legem in timorem, sed liberae secundum Isaac qui *non* accepit *spiritum servitutis in timorem sed adoptionis filiorum clamantem Abba pater.* Qui diligit Deum non timet serviliter. Scriptum est: *Timor non est in dilectione, sed consummata dilectio foras mittit timorem. Quoniam timor poenam habet, qui autem timet non est consummatus in dilectione.* Timor enim servilis cum odio est disciplinae, filii autem cum honore patris.

Aliud est timere ex lege, aliud honorare pro veneratione tremendae Dei maiestatis. Eiusmodi similes sunt patri suo qui in caelis est, commemorati et edocti amant bonum oderunt malum. Non metu fugiunt malum, non necessitate faciunt bonum; sine lege sunt, liberi sunt, ipsi promissi sunt. Non ipsis dicitur *Si me audieritis.* Cui dicitur *Si me audieritis* potest et non audire; numquid convenit in eum quem Deus ante

condition, i.e., the law, was only given to the impious and to sinners, to the end that they might either flee to grace or else be punished all the more justly if they disregard it.

What is the point of the law for the just, for whom "the law was not laid down?"[1] They have God's favor and do the law without any law; they serve God freely and live according to the image and likeness of God and of Christ. They are good because that is what they want. It is fear of death, however, that keeps the person who is subject to the law from openly committing murder. Such a person is not merciful, is no image of God.[2] He finds no pleasure in the law, but only fears the punishment it inflicts. He cannot perform what he thinks that necessity rather than conviction compels him to do. The person who does not join his soul to God's will is inevitably given over to his own will and shall certainly receive the reward due to his will. What God has willed is displeasing to him. For anyone who is good by necessity is evil by will. The law acts as a constraint on the deed, not on the will. No one who would follow the evil, if only evil had no penalty, is conjoined to God. No one does God's will, if he groans at not doing his own. And no one is merciful, if he is simply afraid to be cruel. He is under the law; he is a slave. He does not hate theft; he fears its penalty. Persuaded and overcome, he inevitably steals because he is carnal and under the power of sin, not having the Spirit of God. But the person who loves the good is God's image and lives by faith in the Lord; he is no longer heir as a son of the slave who receives the law in fear, but as a son of the free woman, like Isaac, who "did not receive the spirit of slavery in fear, but the spirit of adoption as sons, crying, Abba, Father."[3] The person who loves God has no servile fear. It is written: "there is no fear in love, but perfect love casts out fear. For fear has to do with punishment, and he who fears has not been perfected in love."[4] Servile fear is a matter of hating discipline, a son's fear is a matter of honoring his father.

It is one thing to be afraid on account of the law, and quite another to give honor out of veneration for God's awesome majesty. Such people are like their father who is in heaven; once reminded and instructed, they love the good and hate the evil. They do not flee the evil out of fear or do the good out of necessity. And they are without the law; they are free. They are the ones who were promised. They are not the ones to whom, "if you obey me,"[5] is addressed. "If you obey me" is addressed to the person who is also able not to obey. How can it pertain to the person of

---

[1] 1 Tim. 1:9

[2] Possibly an allusion to Lk. 6:36: "Be merciful even as your father is merciful."

[3] Rom. 8:15

[4] 1 Jn. 4:18

[5] Is. 1:19

mundum praevidit auditurum? Et iusti quidem *quos* Deus *praescivit* sunt in ista lege. Dicitur et ipsis *Si me audieritis*, sed alia causa, non quia possunt non audire, sed ut semper solliciti sint suae salutis, incerti exitus sui. Non enim securus est unusquisque ex numero se esse praescitorum, apostolo dicente: *Ne ipse reprobus fiam.* Non est ergo illis irae operatrix ista lex sed fidei exercitium, quo iugiter Dei gratiam quaerant laborantes ut perficiatur quod in illis Deus praevidit, et de libero arbitrio fuerint ad vitam destinati. Alias impossibile est non audire eum quem Deus auditurum praevidit, promisit, iuravit.

In quam vero partem lex proprie conveniat, licet uni detur corpori, Dominus in Evangelio declarat dicens apostolis: *Si haec scitis beati estis si feceritis ea. Non de omnibus uobis dico; ego scio quos elegi.* Magna breuitas ostendentis unum corpus et separantis! Si enim diceret: Non de uobis dico, aut: Non de omnibus dico, non ostenderet unum corpus. Nunc autem *non omnibus uobis dico* ostendit quia et si non de omnibus de illis tamen dixit, sicut quis dicat Non de toto te dixi. Duo autem corpora mixta sunt velut unum, et in commune unum corpus laudatur aut increpatur. Sicut in Exodo, cum quidam contra vetitum sabbati exissent manna colligere, ait Deus Moysi: *Quousque non uultis audire legem meum*, cum Moses semper audierit?

Quid de illa lege dicemus quae aperte promissioni videtur adversa? Sicut scriptum est in Esaia: *Si me audisses Israhel, esset sicut harena maris numerus tuus.* Ecce increpatur Israhel quod vitio suo non fuerit factus sicut harena. Superest intellegere quia si semper non audierit semper exiguus erit. Et ubi firmitas promissionum? Sed hoc fit quia prius volumus intellegere quam credere et fidem rationi subicere. Si autem credamus omni modo ita fieri ut Deus iuravit, dabit rationem fides quam perfidum est rationem quaerere, et intellegemus firmitatem magis esse promissionum quam putamus infirmitatem. Hoc enim dictum *si me audisses Israhel* commemoratio est iustitiae Dei et conformatio promissionum, ne quis putaret non libero arbitrio sed dispositione Dei quosdam

whom God foresaw, even before the world began, that he would obey? To be sure, the just "whom God foreknew"[1] are also under that law. To them also, "if you obey me" is addressed; but for a different reason: not because they are able not to obey, but to the end that they might always be anxious about their own salvation, uncertain about their own destiny. For no one is certain that he is of the number of the foreknown, since even the apostle says, "lest I should myself be rejected."[2] For them, therefore, that law does not work wrath; rather it arouses faith so that they constantly seek God's grace and work to the end that what God foresaw in them might be perfected and, by free will, they might be destined to life. This apart, not to obey is impossible for the person of whom God foresaw, promised and swore that he would obey.

Although the law is given to the one body, the Lord makes clear to which part it properly pertains when, in the gospel, he tells the apostles, "if you know these things, blessed are you if you do them. I am not speaking of you all; I know those whom I have chosen."[3] How concisely he both displays the one body and divides it. If he were to say, "I am not speaking of you," or "I am not speaking of all," he would not display the one body. But now, by saying, "I am not speaking of you all," he shows that even if he did not speak of them all, he did speak of them. It is as if someone were to say, "I did not speak of you as a whole." The two bodies have been joined as one; and the one body is praised or blamed in common. So also in Exodus, when some had gone out to gather manna against the sabbath ban, God said to Moses, "how long do you refuse to obey my law?"[4]—even though Moses himself always obeyed.

What shall we say of that law which seems plainly to run counter to the promise? It is written in Isaiah: "if you had obeyed me, Israel, your number would have been like the sand of the sea."[5] See how Israel is blamed because, by its own fault, it has not become like the sand. We are left to understand that if Israel never obeys it will always be small. And where is the firmness of the promises? But this question arises because we want to understand before we believe and to make faith subject to reason. But if we believe that the outcome will most certainly be as God swore that it would be, faith will give us the reason which it is perfidious for reason to seek, and we will understand that the firmness of the promises is greater than the weakness we imagined them to have. This saying, "if you had obeyed me, Israel," is a reminder of God's justice and a configuration of the promises designed to keep anyone from thinking that it is by divine disposition, rather than by free will, that some are

---

[1] Rom. 8:29
[2] 1 Cor. 9:27
[3] Jn. 13:17-18
[4] Ex. 16:28
[5] Is. 48:18, 19

factos ad mortem quosdam vero ad vitam. Propterea praesentibus dixit *si me audissetis*, ut manifestum fieret post promisit, ut harenam futuros quia praevidit audituros. Ante Dominum enim Christum, cum de hoc dictum est, numquam fuit semen Abrahae sicut harena maris. Quod probare facile est. Primum quia in Christo promisit hanc multitudinem: *Non in seminibus quasi in multis sed quasi in uno, et semini tuo quod est Christus.* Deinde quia omnes gentes promisit, quod ante Christum fieri non potuit. Et si fuit ante Dominum numerus filiorum Israhel sicut harena maris, sed cum falsis fratribus qui non sunt filii Abrahae. Non enim quia omnes ex Abraham omnes filii Abrahae aut quia ex Israhel ii Israhel. Sicut apostolus, cum se *anathema optaret* pro Israhel *quorum* esset *filiorum adoptio* et *testamenta*, ostendit non esse huiusmodi filios Abrahae, sed de affectu carnalis necessitudinis doleret quod ex ipso numero non essent, non quod promissio Dei excidisset, dicens: *Non tamen excidit sermo Dei, non enim omnes qui sunt ex Israhel hi sunt Israhel neque quia sunt semen Abrahae omnes filii, sed in Isaac vocabitur tibi semen; id est non qui sunt filii carnis hi sunt filii Dei, sed filii promissionis deputantur in semen.* Ergo in antiqua multitudine non fuit Abrahae semen, nisi illi qui secundum Isaac fidei et promissionis filii erant. Etiam hoc exemplum inducit: *Si fuerit numerus filiorum Israhel sicut harena maris, reliquiae liberabuntur*, id est exiguum. Et: *Nisi Dominus Sabaoth reliquisset nobis semen sicut Sodoma essemus.* Ipsae reliquiae fuerunt semen Abrahae, ne omnis Iudaea ut Sodoma esset. Iterum cum assereret numquam Deum hereditatem suam reliquisse sed sicut in adventu Domini pars Israhel salva facta est ita semper fuisse. *Quid* inquit *dicit responsum? Reliqui mihi septem milia virorum qui non curvaverunt genua Bahal. Sic nunc reliquiae secundum electionem gratiae salvae factae sunt.* Dicendo *sic nunc in hoc tempore* ostendit et ante sic factum in Israhel ut reliquiae, id est modicum, salvum fieret.

Si autem nec fides nec ratio persuadet, sed ei qui promissus fuerat dictum est: *Si me audisses Israhel, esset sicut harena maris numerus tuus.* Et

made for death, some for life. To those present he said, "if you had obeyed me," precisely so that it would be manifest, after he made the promise, that they would become like the sand because he foresaw that they would obey. Before the Lord Christ, when this was said about him, the descendants of Abraham were never like the sand of the sea. This point is easily proved: first, because he promised this multitude in Christ: "not in offsprings, as referring to many, but, as referring to one, in your offspring, which is Christ";[1] then, because he promised all the nations, and this[2] could not occur before Christ. And even if the number of the children of Israel was like the sand of the sea before the Lord came, that number included false brethren who are not sons of Abraham. For it is not true that, because they all stem from Abraham, they are all sons of Abraham or that, because they come from Israel, they belong to Israel. When the apostle wished himself accursed for the sake of Israel, to whom belong the "adoption as sons" and the "covenants,"[3] he showed that they were not sons of Abraham in this sense. Moved by human distress, he grieved because they were not of that number, but not because God's promise had failed. As he said: "yet the word of God has not failed, for not all who come from Israel belong to Israel, nor are all sons just because they are descended from Abraham, but in Isaac will your line be named; that is, it is not the sons of the flesh who are the sons of God, but rather the sons of the promise are reckoned as the true descendants."[4] Therefore the ancient multitude did not include Abraham's line apart from those who, like Isaac, were sons of faith and the promise. He also introduces this instance: "though the number of the sons of Israel be as the sand of the sea, a remnant will be saved,"[5] i.e., a few. And: "if the Lord of hosts had not left us descendants, we would have been like Sodom."[6] That remnant was Abraham's line, preserved lest Judaea should have been like Sodom. Again, he asserts that God has never abandoned his inheritance; rather just as, at the Lord's advent, a part of Israel was saved, so it had always been. "What," he says, "is his reply? I have kept for myself seven thousand men who have not bent the knee to Baal. So now a remnant, chosen by grace, has been saved."[7] By saying, "so now in this time," he showed that it had also happened before in Israel that a remnant, i.e., a few, was saved.

But if neither faith nor reason persuades, and it was to the one who had been promised that it was said, "if you had obeyed me, Israel, your

---

[1]Gal. 3:16

[2]I.e., the coming of all the nations.

[3]Rom. 9:3, 4

[4]Rom. 9:6-8

[5]Rom. 9:27

[6]Rom. 9:29

[7]Rom. 11:4-5

Iacob qui ante quam nasceretur electus est, idem de libero arbitrio post modum reprobatus est, sicut Osee dicit: *Iudicium Domini ad Iudam ut vindicet in Iacob secundum vias eius, et secundum studia eius retribuet ei.* Quia *In utero supplantavit fratrem suum et in laboribus suis invaluit ad Deum, et invaluit cum angelo et potens factus est.* Si autem constat in Iacob dilectum consummasse, non est idem qui *in laboribus invaluit ad Deum et supplantator,* sed duo in uno corpore. Figura est enim duplicis seminis Abrahae, id est duorum populorum in uno utero matris Ecclesiae luctantium. Unus est secundum electionem de praescientia dilectus, alter electione suae voluntatis iniquus.

Iacob autem et Esau in uno sunt corpore ex uno semine sed quod perspicue duo procreati sunt *ostensio* est *duorum* populorum. Et ne quis putaret ita perspicue fore separatos duos populos, ostensum est ambos in uno corpore futuros in Iacob, qui et *dilectus* vocatus est et *fratris supplantator* expressus. Itaque in duobus quantitas expressa est non qualitas separationis. Ceterum ambo qui separati sunt in uno futuri ante quam dividuntur ostensi sunt. Et Isaac *Venit* inquit *frater tuus cum dolo et accepit benedictionem.* Nisi ista locutio mystica sit breuiter ostendentis duo in uno corpore, nonne contra rationem est ut benedictionem in proximum dolosus acceperit, Scriptura dicente: *Qui non iuravit proximo suo in dolo, iste accipiet benedictionem a Domino?* Numquam autem Iacob, id est Ecclesia, venit ad benedictionem non comitante dolo, id est falsis fratribus. Sed non quia innocentia et dolus simul veniunt ad benedictionem simul benedicentur, quia *qui potest capere* capit, et unum semen pro qualitate terrae provenit.

Non est autem contrarium quod malum fratrem videtur supplantasse, quia non dixit *in utero supplantavit Esau* sed *fratrem suum.* Esau autem ubique signum est et nomen malorum, Iacob autem utrorumque, illa ratione quod pars mala simulet se Iacob et sint duo sub uno nomine. Pars autem bona non potest se simulare Esau: inde est hoc nomen malorum tantem, illud vero bipertitum. Ceterum de libero arbitrio nec Iacob omne

number would have been as the sand of the sea," then note: so too the same Jacob who was chosen before his birth[1] was later rejected as the result of his free will, as Hosea says: "the Lord's judgment against Judah, that he will punish Jacob for his ways and will repay him for his pursuits" because "he supplanted his brother in the womb and in his striving he prevailed against God and prevailed with the angel and grew strong."[2] But if it is true that he had already consummated his love for Jacob, then this Jacob is not the same Jacob who "in his striving prevailed against God" and was a supplanter. Rather there were two in one body. For this is a figure of the double line of Abraham's descendants, i.e., of two peoples wrestling in the one womb of their mother, the church. The one, chosen on the basis of foreknowledge, is loved; the other, by the choice of its own will, is evil.

Moreover Jacob and Esau are in one body and come from one line of descent; but the fact that they clearly came to birth as two individuals shows forth the two peoples. Yet, lest anyone think, as a result, that the two peoples would be sharply separated, it was made plain that both would be in one body, in Jacob who was both said to be "loved" and termed a "supplanter of his brother." In the two, therefore, a quantity is expressed, not a quality of separation. Thus it was shown that the two separate individuals were going to remain in one body until the time when they are finally distinguished from each other. Isaac said, "your brother came deceitfully and received the blessing."[3] Unless this is a mystic expression on the part of someone showing us, in brief, the two in one body, it can only run counter to reason that someone who deceives his neighbor should receive the blessing. Scripture says: "he who has not sworn deceitfully to his neighbor, he will receive blessing from the Lord."[4] Yet Jacob, i.e., the church, never comes for blessing without concomitant deceit, i.e., without false brethren. But the fact that innocence and deceit come for blessing together does not mean that they are blessed together, for "he who is able to receive"[5] receives and the one seed grows up according to the quality of the ground.[6]

It is no objection that he seems to have supplanted the evil brother, for it did not say, "he supplanted Esau in the womb," but "his brother." Esau is invariably a sign and name for the evil, but Jacob for both. The reason is that the evil part decks itself out as Jacob and the two appear under one name. But the good part is unable to deck itself out as Esau. Consequently Esau is a name for the evil only; but Jacob is bipartite. Besides, as a

---

[1]The allusion is to Rom. 9:11-13.

[2]Hos. 12:2-4

[3]Gen. 27:35

[4]Ps. 24:4-5

[5]Mt. 19:12

[6]Apparently an allusion to the parable of the sower (Mt. 13:1-9, 18-23).

semen bonum nec Esau omne malum, sed ex utroque utrumque. Ex Abraham ita bipertitum semen ostensum est. Natum est unum ex ancilla in figura, ut ostenderetur et servos futuros ex Abraham, et recessit cum sua matre. Post quam vero recessit inventum est in alterius semine, quod est ex libera, quod est ex Israhel qui accepit legem *in monte Sina, quod est Agar in servitutem generans.* Illic in eodem populo secundum Isaac ex libera *promissionis filii,* id est sancti et fideles, multi procreati sunt. Separatis itaque a credentibus figuris Ismahel et Esau, in uno populo totum post modum provenit. Illic ab origine utrumque testamentum Agar et Isaac, sed pro tempore alterum sub alterius nomine, delituit et delitescit, quia neque revelato novo quiescit vetus generando. Non enim dixit *Agar quae in senectute generavit,* sed *Quae est Agar in servitutem generans.*

Oportet autem *ambos simul crescere usque ad messem.* Sicut ergo tunc sub professione veteris testamenti latuit novum, id est gratia quae secundum Isaac promissionis filios generaret ex libera, quod in Christo revelatum est; ita et nunc obtinente novo non desunt servitutis filii generante Agar, quod Christo iudicante revelabitur. Confirmat apostolus id nunc quoque inter fratres geri quod tunc inter illos gerebatur dicens. *Vos autem fratres secundum Isaac promissionis filii estis. Sed sicut tunc qui secundum carnem natus est persequebatur spiritalem, ita et nunc.* Et necessario addidit: *Quid dicit Scriptura? Expelle ancillam et filium eius, non enim coheres erit filius ancillae cum filio liberae.* Quod autem dixit *sicut tunc persequebatur ita et nunc,* non est inane. Apostolus enim interpretatus est *persequebatur.* Nam Scriptura dicit: *Ludebat* Ismahel *cum Isaac.* Numquid fratres qui circumcisionem Galatis praedicabant aperte illos et non per lusum, id est sine indicio persecutionis, insequabantur? Sicut ergo Ismahel genere ludendi persecutorem dixit, ita et istos, qui filios Dei velut per communem utilitatem, id est disciplinam legis, a Christo separare et matris suae Agar filios facere militant.

consequence of free will, Jacob does not represent all the good line of descent, nor Esau all the evil. Rather both include both. Thus it was shown that a bipartite line came from Abraham. The one was born from the slave in a figure, in order to show that there would be slaves from Abraham's line, and he departed with his mother. But after he departed, he was found in the other's line, which is from the free woman, which is from Israel who received the law "on Mount Sinai, which is Hagar bearing children for slavery."[1] There, in the same people, many "children of promise"[2]—i.e., saints and believers—were begotten, like Isaac, from the free women. Thus, although the figures of Ishmael and Esau had been separated from the faithful, the whole emerged afterwards in one people. From the beginning both covenants, Hagar and Isaac, although the one under the other's name for the time being, lay hidden there—and still lie hidden, for the fact that the new covenant has been revealed does not mean that the old has ceased to bear children. For he did not say, "Hagar who gave birth in her old age," but, "which is Hagar bearing children for slavery."

And it is right that "both grow together until the harvest."[3] Before the new covenant—i.e., the grace which bears children of the promise, like Isaac—was revealed in Christ, it lay hidden under the profession of the old covenant; and now, when the new obtains, Hagar continues to give birth and there is no lack of children of slavery, as will be revealed when Christ returns as judge. The apostle confirms that what once took place among them still takes place now among the brethren, when he says: "now you, brethren, like Isaac, are children of promise. But as at that time the child born according to the flesh persecuted the child born spiritually, so it is now." And of necessity he adds, "what does scripture say? Drive out the slave and her son, for the son of the slave will not be co-heir with the son of the free woman."[4] Nor is it without foundation that he said, "as at that time he persecuted, so it is now." For the apostle has explained "he persecuted." Scripture says that Ishmael "was playing with Isaac."[5] Did the brethren who were preaching circumcision to the Galatians assault them openly? Or did they do it through play, i.e., without any open indication of persecution? Therefore, just as he called Ishmael a persecutor with respect to his play, so also he calls those people persecutors who fight to separate the sons of God from Christ and strive to make them sons of Hagar, their own mother, by appealing to what is of common use, i.e., the discipline of the law.

---

[1]Gal. 4:24
[2]Gal. 4:28
[3]Mt. 13:30
[4]Gal. 4:28-30
[5]Gen. 21:9

Alia enim non est causa qua filii diaboli irrepant *ad explorandum libertatem nostram,* et simulent se fratres et in paradiso nostro velut Dei filios ludere, quam ut de subacta libertate filiorum Dei glorientur; *qui portabant iudicium qualescumque illi fuerint,* qui omnem sanctum persecuti sunt, qui prophetas occiderunt, qui *semper Spiritui Sancto restiterunt; inimici crucis Christi, negantes Christum in carne* dum eius membra oderunt, corpus *peccati, fillus exterminii* in *mysterium facinoris,* qui veniunt *secundum operationem Satanae in omni virtute signis et prodigiis falsitatis, spiritalia nequitiae in caelestibus,* quos *Dominus* Christus quem in carne persecuntur *interficiet spiritu oris sui et destruet manifestatione adventus sui.* Tempus est enim quo haec non in mysteriis sed aperte dicantur, imminente *discessione* quod est revelatio *hominis peccati,* discedente Loth a Sodomis.

IV. De specie et genere

De specie et genere loquimur, non secundum artem rhetoricam humanae sapientiae, quam qui magis omnibus potuit locutus non est, *ne crucem Christi* fecisset *inanem* si auxilio atque ornamento sermonis ut falsitas indiguisset. Sed loquimur secundum mysteria caelestis sapientiae magisterio Spiritus Sancti, qui cum veritatis pretium fidem constituerit mysteriis narravit in speciem genus abscondens, ut in veterem Hierusalem totam quae nunc est per orbem, aut in unum membrum totum corpus ut in Salomone. Sed hoc tam occultum est quam cetera quae non solum specie breuiante sed etiam multiformi narratione occultantur. Quam ob rem Dei gratia in auxilium postulata elaborandum

For the only reason why the children of the devil steal in "to spy on our liberty"[1] and pretend to be brothers at play in our paradise, as if they were children of God, is to boast that the liberty of God's children has been undermined.   They brought judgment, no matter who they were;[2] they persecuted every saint; they killed the prophets;[3] they "always resisted the Holy Spirit";[4] "enemies of Christ's cross,"[5] "denying that Christ came in the flesh"[6] while they hated his members, the body of sin, "the son of perdition" in "the mystery of lawlessness," they come "by Satan's work with all power and with false signs and wonders";[7] they are "the spiritual hosts of wickedness in the heavens,"[8] whom "the Lord" Christ, whom they persecuted in the flesh, "will kill with the breath of his mouth and destroy when he comes in open manifestation."[9] For there is a time when these things may be said not in riddles but openly, as that "departure" approaches which is the revelation of the "man of sin,"[10] when Lot departs from Sodom.[11]

IV. The Particular and the General

I am not referring to the particular and the general as they are used in the rhetorical art devised by human wisdom.[12]   Although better able than anyone, Paul did not use that art—for fear that he would have made "the cross of Christ empty"[13] if, like falsehood, it needed the aid and ornament of eloquence.   Rather I am speaking with reference to the mysteries of heavenly wisdom in relation to the teaching of the Holy Spirit.   Making faith the price of truth, the Spirit produced an account marked by mysteries, concealing the general in the particular: for instance, the whole city, now spread throughout the world, in the old Jerusalem or the whole body in a single member such as Solomon. But this was hidden, as were the other things which are hidden not only by abridgment in the particular but also by the multiform character of the narrative.   On this account, having asked the help of God's grace, we

---

[1]Gal. 2:4

[2]The allusion is to Gal. 5:10.

[3]The allusions are to Acts 7:52 and Mt. 23:37.

[4]Acts 7:51

[5]Phil. 3:18

[6]1 Jn. 2:22, 4:3

[7]2 Thess. 2:3, 7, 9

[8]Eph. 6:12

[9]2 Thess. 2:8

[10]2 Thess. 2:3

[11]There seems to be a double allusion here: to Lk. 17:29-30 and to Gen. 19:29.

[12]See, for example, Quintilian *Institutio Oratorica* 7.1.23-28.

[13]1 Cor. 1:17

Liber Regularum Tyconii

nobis est, et *Spiritus multiplicis ingressus* legendi eloquiumque *subtile,* quo, dum ad impedimentum intellectus speciei genus aut generi speciem inserit, genus speciesne sit facile videri possit. Dum enim speciem narrat ita in genus transit ut transitus non statim liquido appareat, sed talia transiens ponit uerba quae in utrumque conveniant, donec paulatim speciei modum excedat et transitus dilucidetur, cum quae ab specie coeperant non nisi in genus convenerint. Et eodem modo genus relinquit in speciem rediens.

Aliquando autem ab specie in genus non supradicto modo sed evidenter transit et supradicto more revertitur. Aliquando supradicto modo transit et evidenter revertitur simili ordinis varietate, aut ab specie in genere aut a genere in specie finit narrationem. Aliquando redit ex hoc in illud non semel, et omnis narratio nec speciem excedit nec genus praeterit in utrumque conveniens. Haec varietas translationis et ordinis exigit fidem quae gratiam Dei quaerat.

Sic Deus per Ezechielem loquitur et regressui eorum qui ab Hierusalem capti et disparsi fuerunt gentium iungit adventum, et in terra quam patres nostri possiderant exprimit mundum. Septem enim gentes Abrahae promissae figura est omnium gentium. *Factus est* inquit *ad me sermo Domini dicens: fili hominis, domus Israhel habitavit in terra et polluerunt illam in via sua et in idolis suis et peccatis suis; secundum immunditiam menstruatae facta est via eorum ante faciem meam. Et effudi iram meam super eos, et disparsi illos inter nationes et ventilavi eos in regiones secundum vias eorum et secundum peccata eorum iudicavi eos. Et ingressi sunt inter nationes quas ingressi sunt illic, et polluerunt nomen meum sanctum, dum dicunt ipsi Populus Domini hic, et de terra sui egressi sunt. Et peperci illis propter nomen meum sanctum quod polluerunt domus Israhel in nationibus in quas ingressi sunt illic. Propter hoc dic domui Israhel: haec dicit Dominus, non vobis ego facio domus Israhel, sed propter nomen meum sanctum quod polluistis in nationibus in medio in quas ingressi sunt illic.* Incipit iungere genus: *Et sanctificabo nomen meum sanctum illud magnum quod pollutum est inter nationes quod polluistis in medio earum, et scient*

must spell out the "entries"[1] into reading and the "subtle" discourse of the "manifold Spirit"[2] so that, when he inserts the general into the particular or the particular into the general as an obstacle to understanding, we can easily see whether we are dealing with the particular or the general. For, while relating the particular, he passes over into the general in such a way that the transition is not immediately clear. Rather, in making the transition, he uses words that are appropriate to both until, little by little, he exceeds the mode of the particular, and the transition becomes plain to see. What had begun with the particular now fits only the general. And when he returns to the particular, he moves away from the general in the same manner.

Sometimes, however, he passes from the particular to the general not in the manner just described, but quite obviously, and then returns in the described fashion. Sometimes he makes the transition as described and returns quite obviously. With a similar variety of pattern, he may conclude in the general an account that began with the particular or conclude in the particular one that began with the general. Sometimes he does not altogether turn from the one to the other, and the whole narrative neither exceeds the particular nor omits the general but pertains to both. This variety of transition and order is what exacts the faith that seeks God's grace.

It is in this fashion that God speaks through Ezekiel. He links the coming of the gentiles to the return of the captives who had been taken from Jerusalem and scattered abroad; and he uses the land which our fathers had possessed to represent the world. For the seven nations[3] promised to Abraham are a figure for all the nations "The word of the Lord," he says, "came to me and said: son of man, the house of Israel lived in the land and defiled it with their conduct and their idols and their sins. Their conduct before me was like the uncleanness of a menstruating woman. And I poured out my wrath upon them and scattered them among the nations and dispersed them to far quarters. I judged them according to their conduct and their sins. And they entered the nations where they went; and they defiled my holy name so long as the nations said, these are the people of the Lord and they have gone out from their own land. Yet I spared them for the sake of my holy name which the house of Israel defiled in the nations where they went. Say, therefore, to the house of Israel: thus says the Lord: I am not doing this for you, house of Israel, but for the sake of my holy name which you have defiled

---

[1]Ecclus. 1.7 (cf. Vulgate)

[2]Wisd. 7:22

[3]See Deut. 7:1 and Acts 13:19.

gentes quoniam ego sum Dominus, dum sanctificor in vobis ante oculos eorum, et accipiam vos de gentibus et congregabo vos ex omnibus terris et inducam vos in terram vestram. Aperte excedit speciem: *Et aspergam vos aquam mundam et mundabimini ab omnibus simulacris vestris, et mundabo vos et dabo vobis cor novum, et spiritum novum dabo in vobis, et auferam cor lapideum de carne vestra et dabo vobis cor carneum, et spiritum meum dabo in vos, et faciam ut in iustitiis meis ambuletis et iudicia mea custodiatis et faciatis. Et habitabitis in terra quam dedi patribus vestris, et eritis mihi in populum et ego ero vobis in Deum, et mundabo vos ex omnibus immunditiis vestris.* Adtingit speciem non tamen relinquens genus: *Et vocabo triticum et multiplicabo illud et non dabo in vos famem, et multiplicabo fructum ligni et quae nascuntur in agro, ut non accipiatis ultra opprobrium famis in nationibus. Et reminiscemini vias vestras pessimas et cogitationes vestras non bonas, et odio habebitis eas ante faciem eorum in iniquitatibus vestris et in abominationibus eorum. Non propter vos ego facio, dicit Dominus; notum est vobis, confundimini et revertimini de viis vestris, domus Israhel. Haec dicit Adonai Dominus: in die qua mundabo vos ab omnibus inquitatibus vestris et inhabitari faciam civitates*—in figura terrae Iudae quae bellis vastata fuerat promittit innovari mundum qui a Deo recesserat—*et reaedificabuntur deserta et terra quae exterminata fuerit coletur, propter quod fuit exterminata sub oculis omnis praetereuntis. Et dicent: Terra illa quae fuerat exterminata facta est sicut hortus deliciarum, et civitates desertae et demolitae munitae consederunt. Et scient gentes quaecumque derelictae fuerint in circuitu vestro quia ego sum Dominus. Aedificavi demolitas et plantavi exterminatas, quia ego Dominus locutus sum et feci.*

Apostolus quoque in ingressu Iacob promissum esse introitum gentium sic interpretatur dicens: *Donec plenitudo gentium intret, et sic omnis Israhel salvabitur. Sicut scriptum est: Veniet a Sion qui liberet et auferet impietates ab Iacob,* et eodem genere locutionis redit in speciem dicens: *Secundum*

in the midst[1] of the nations where you have gone." Here he begins to bring in the general: "I will sanctify my holy name, the great name which has been defiled among the nations, which you have defiled in their midst. And the nations will know that I am the Lord when I am sanctified in you before their eyes. I will take you from the nations and gather you from all the lands and lead you into your own land." Now he openly goes beyond the particular: "And I will sprinkle clean water over you, and you will be cleansed from all your idols. And I will cleanse you and will give you a new heart and will put a new spirit in you. I will take the heart of stone from your flesh and will give you a heart of flesh and will put my spirit in you. And I will cause you to walk in my statutes and to keep my ordinances and do them. And you will dwell in the land which I gave to your fathers; and you will be my people, and I will be your God, and I will cleanse you from all your uncleanness." Now he touches on the particular, but without leaving the general: "And I will summon the grain and multiply it and will bring no famine among you. And I will multiply the fruit on the tree and the growth in the field so that you no longer have to bear the indignity of famine among the nations. And you will remember your evil ways and your ill-aimed designs; and you will hate them before the nations for your iniquities and for their abominations. Not for your sake am I doing this, says the lord; it is known to you, be ashamed and turn back from your ways, house of Israel. Thus says the Lord God: on the day when I will cleanse you from all your iniquities, I will also repopulate the cities"—under the figure of the land of Judah, which had been laid waste by wars, he promises to renew the world which had departed from God—"and the ruins will be rebuilt and the wasteland will be cultivated, since it was a wasteland for every passer-by to see. And they will say: the land that was a wasteland has become like a garden of delights, and the abandoned and ruined cities have been fortified and established. And any nations left around you will know that I am the Lord. I have rebuilt the ruins and replanted the wastelands, because I, the Lord, have spoken and I have done it."[2]

The apostle also indicates in this fashion that the entry of the gentiles was promised in the return of Jacob, when he says: "until the full number of the gentiles comes in, and so all Israel will be saved. As it is written: the deliverer will come from Zion and will take impiety from Jacob"; and, using the same kind of expression, he returns to the

---

[1]The phrases "in the midst" and "from the midst," which occur in several of the passages Tyconius cites, would almost certainly suggest 2 Thess. 2:7 to his mind; and the link is important as it intimates a connection between his view of the present condition of the church and his view of the eschatological "departure" of the church from its current "bipartite" situation "in the midst" of the world.

[2]Ezek. 36:16-36

Evangelium quidem inimici propter vos.

Item in Ezechiele incipit ab specie quae conveniat et in genus, et finit in solo genere ostendens terram patrum mundi esse possessionem. *Haec dicit Dominus, Ecce ego accipiam omnem domum Israhel de medio gentium in quas ingressi sunt illic, et congregabo eos ab omnibus qui sunt in circuitu eorum et inducam eos in terram Israhel. Et dabo eos in gentem in terra mea et in montibus Israhel, et princeps unus erit eorum. Et non erunt ultra in duas gentes nec dividentur ultra in duo regna, ne contaminentur adhuc in simulacris suis. Et liberabo eos ab omnibus iniquitatibus eorum quibus peccaverunt in eis, et emundabo eos, et erunt mihi in populum et ego Dominus ero illis in Deum.* Aperte transit in genus: *Et servus meus David princeps in medio eorum erit, pastor unus omnium qui in praeceptis meis ambulabunt et iudicia mea custodient et facient ea. Et inhabitabunt in terra sua quam ego dedi servo meo Iacob ubi habitaverint patres eorum, et inhabitabunt in ea ipsi, et David servus meus princeps eorum in saecula. Et disponam illis testamentum pacis et testamentum aeternum erit cum illis, et ponam sancta mea in medio eorum in saecula et erit habitatio mea in eis, et ero illis Deus et ipsi erunt mihi populus. Et scient gentes quia ego sum Dominus qui sanctifico eos, dum sunt sancti in medio eorum in saecula, dicit Dominus.*

Item illic regressui dispersionis Israhel gentium inserit adventum, et Aegypti heremum figuram populi deserti in quo Ecclesia nunc esse manifestatur, et quod idem mali, quamvis una cum populo Dei ex gentibus revocentur in terram Israhel, tamen in terra Israhel non sint. *Vivo ego dicit Dominus si respondero vobis, et si ascenderit in spiritum vestrum hoc. Et non erit quem ad modum dicitis vos: Erimus sicut gentes et sicut tribus terrae ut serviamus lignis et lapidibus. Vivo ego, dicit Dominus, nisi in manu forti et brachio excelso et in ira effusa regnabo super vos, et educam vos de populis et recipiam vos de regionibus in quibus dispersi estis in manu forti et brachio excelso et in ira effusa, et adducam vos in desertum populorum, et disputabo illic ad vos facie ad faciem, quem ad modum disputavi ad patres vestros in deserto terrae Aegypti sic iudicabo vos, dicit Dominus. Et redigam vos sub virgam meam et inducam vos in numero, et eligam impios de vobis et desertores, quoniam ex transmigratione eorum*

particular where he says: "with regard to the gospel, to be sure, they are enemies for your sake."[1]

Again, in Ezekiel, he begins with a particular which also pertains to the general and ends in the general alone, showing that the land of our fathers represents the possession of the world. "Thus says the Lord: behold, I will take all the house of Israel from the midst of the nations where they went, and I will gather them from all who are around them and will lead them into the land of Israel. And I will make them a nation in my land and on the mountains of Israel, and they will have one ruler. And they will no longer be separated into two nations or divided in two kingdoms, lest they continue to contaminate themselves with their idols. And I will deliver them from all the iniquities with which they have sinned among the nations; and I will cleanse them, and they will be my people and I, the Lord, will be their God." Now he openly passes over into the general: "and my servant David will be ruler among them, the one shepherd of all who walk in my precepts and keep my statutes and do them. And they will dwell in their own land, which I gave to my servant Jacob, the land where their fathers dwelt; and they will dwell in it themselves, and my servant David will be their ruler for ever. And I will make a covenant of peace with them; and it will be an eternal covenant with them. I will put my sanctuary among them for ever, and my dwelling place will be with them; and I will be their God, and they will be my people. And the nations will know that I am the Lord, the one who sanctifies them, when the saints are in their midst for ever, says the Lord."[2]

There, again, he treats the coming of the gentiles in the return of Israel from its dispersion; and it is made clear that the desert of Egypt is a figure of the forsaken people among whom the church now exists and that these same evil people, although called back from the nations into the land of Israel together with the people of God, are not actually in the land of Israel. "As I live, says the Lord, I will not answer you and this will not come into your mind. You say: we will be like the nations and like the tribes of the earth and will worship trees and stones. It will not be so. As I live, says the Lord, I will rule over you with a strong hand and an upraised arm and an outpouring of wrath. With a strong hand and an upraised arm and an outpouring of wrath, I will lead you out from the peoples and take you from the far quarters where you were dispersed. And I will lead you into the desert of peoples; and there I will dispute with you face to face. As I disputed with your fathers in the desert of the land of Egypt, so I will judge you, says the Lord. And I will make you pass under my rod and will bring you in by number; and I will weed out the impious and the deserters among you, for I will bring

---

[1]Rom. 11:25-26, 28
[2]Ezek. 37:21-28

educam eos et in terram Israhel non intrabunt, et cognoscetis quia ego sum Dominus.

Item illic captivitati montium Israhel promittit Deus ubertatem et multiplicationem populorum usque in finem. *Quoniam dederunt* inquit *terram tuam sibi in possessionem cum iucunditate inhonorantes animas, ut exterminarent in vastationem; propterea profetare super terram Israhel et dic montibus et collibus et rivis et nemoribus: haec dicit Dominus, Ecce ego in zelo meo et in ira mea locutus sum, propter quod opprobrium gentium portastis. ecce ego levabo manum meam super nationes quae sunt in circuitu vestro, hi iniuriam suam accipient; vestri autem montes Israhel uvam et fructum vestrum manducabit populus meus qui adpropinquat venire. Quia ecce ego super vos et respiciam super vos et colemini et seminabimini, et multiplicabo super vos totam domum Israhel usque in finem, et habitabuntur civitates, et quae desolatae erant aedificabuntur.*

Item illic velut in novissima resurrectione prima significatur. *Locutus est* inquit *ad me Dominus dicens: fili hominis ossa haec omnis domus Israhel est. Ipsi dicunt: arida facta sunt ossa nostra, interiit spes nostra, expiravimus. Propterea profetare et dic: haec dicit Dominus, Ecce ego aperiam monumenta vestra et educam vos de monumentis vestris et inducam vos in terram Israhel, et scietis quia ego Dominus cum aperiam sepulchra vestra et educam de monumentis populum meum, et dabo Spiritum meum in vos et vivetis, et ponam vos super terram vestram et scietis quia ego sum Dominus.* Numquid cum perspicue surrexerimus tunc sciemus Dominum, et non nunc cum per baptisma resurgimus? Aut mortui poterunt dicere: *Arida facta sunt ossa nostra,* aut merito mortuis id promissum esse credamus? Quod est enim sacramenti ne in ambiguum veniret aperuit Deus. Nam de novissima carnis resurrectione neminem Christianum credimus dubitare.

Et Dominus per Iohannem has resurrectiones manifestat dicens: *Amen dico vobis quia qui verbum meum audit et credit ei qui me misit habet vitam aeternam, et in iudicium non venit sed transit de morte ad vitam. Amen dico vobis quoniam venit hora et nunc est quando mortui audient vocem filii Dei et qui audierint vivent. Sicut enim Pater habet vitam in se, sic dedit Filio vitam habere in se. Et potestatem dedit ei et iudicium facere quia filius hominis est.* Iungit novissimam resurrectionem: *Nolite mirari hoc, quia veniet hora in qua omnes qui in monumentis sunt audient vocem filii*

them out from their exile but they will not enter the land of Israel. And you will know that I am the Lord."[1]

There, again, God promises the captive mountains of Israel that they will bear fruit and that their peoples will increase to the end. "Because," he says, "they gleefully took your land as their own possession, holding lives in contempt, in order to lay it waste. Prophesy, therefore, about the land of Israel and say to its mountains and hills and streams and woods: thus says the Lord: behold, in my ardor and my wrath I have spoken, because you have endured the insults of the nations. Behold, I will raise my hand over the nations around you; they will have their own injuries to bear. But you, mountains of Israel, my people will be coming soon and they will eat your grapes and your fruit. For, behold, I am over you and will have regard for you, and you will be tilled and sown. And I will multiply all the house of Israel on you to the end; and the cities will have people and the waste places will be rebuilt."[2]

Again, the first resurrection is signified, so to say, in the last. "The Lord spoke to me," he says, "and said: son of man, these bones are the whole house of Israel. They are saying: our bones have dried up, our hope has perished, we have breathed our last. Prophesy, therefore, and say: thus says the Lord: behold, I will open your tombs and bring you out from your tombs and lead you into the land of Israel. And you will know that I am the Lord, when I open your graves and bring my people out from their tombs; and I will put my Spirit in you, and you will live. And I will put you in your land, and you will know that I am the Lord."[3] Is it when we visibly rise from the dead that we will come to know the Lord, or rather now when we rise again through baptism? Or could the dead really say, "our bones have dried up"? Or is there any reason to believe that this promise was made to the dead? In order to keep something which is a mystery from coming into doubt, God has disclosed it. For, we believe, no Christian has doubts about the final resurrection of the flesh.

The Lord also makes these two resurrections clear in John when he says, "truly I say to you, whoever hears my word and believes him who sent me has eternal life; he does not come into judgment but passes from death to life. Truly I say to you, the hour comes and now is when the dead will hear the voice of the son of God, and those who hear will live. For just as the Father has life in himself, so he has given it to the Son to have life in himself. And he has given him the power to execute judgment, because he is the son of man." Now he brings in the final resurrection: "Do not wonder at this, for the hour will come when all who are in their tombs will hear the voice of the son of God and will

---

[1]Ezek. 20:31-38
[2]Ezek. 36:5-10
[3]Ezek. 37:11-14

Dei, et exient qui bona fecerunt in resurrectionem vitae, qui male fecerunt in resurrectionem iudicii. Primo dixit *Mortui qui audierint vivent,* secundo *Omnes qui in monumentis sunt exient.*

Item quod in uno homine totum corpus significetur, in Regnorum promittit Deus David Salomonem dicens: *Suscitabo semen tuum post te qui erit ex utero tuo et parabo regnum eius. Ipse aedificabit mihi domum.* Ista et in speciem et in genus conveniunt. Excedit speciem dicens: *Et dirigam thronum eius usque in aeternum.* Iterum in utrumque: *Ego ero ei in patrem et ipse erit mihi in filium. Et si venerit iniustitia eius arguam eum in virga hominum et in tactibus filiorum hominum; misericordiam autem meam non auferam ab eo sicut abstuli a quibus abstuli e conspectu meo, et fidelis fiet domus eius.* Iterum excedit speciem: *Et regnum eius usque in aeternum in conspectu meo, et thronus eius erit confirmatus usque in aeternum.* Quod autem videtur in excessu speciei thronum Christi promittere in aeternum, thronum filii hominis promittit, ita corporis Christi, id est Ecclesiae. Non enim propter David promisit Deus regnaturum Christum, qui *ante constitutionem mundi habuit hanc claritatem.* Et per Esaiam sic dicit Deus Christo: *Magnum tibi erit istud, ut voceris puer meus et statuas tribus Iacob et Israhel dispersionem convertas; ecce posui te in testamentum generis in lumen gentium, ut sis in salutem usque in novissimum terrae.* Quid maius filio Dei vocari puerum eius et Israhel dispersionem convertere, aut per eum factum esse ipsum Israhel et caelum et terram et quae in eis sunt visibilia et invisibilia? Sed ei dicit magnum esse qui filio Dei mixtus est ex semine David. Omnis enim promissio Abrahae et David ipsa est, ut semen eorum miscereretur ei cuius sunt omnia, et esset coheres in aeternum, non ut propter ipsos regnaret Christus qui est omnium rex a Patre constitutus.

come forth; those who did good will rise again to life, those who did evil to judgment."[1] First he said, "the dead who hear will live"; second, "all who are in their tombs will come forth."

Again, since the whole body may be signified in one person, God promises David, in Kings, that he will have Solomon: "I will raise up your offspring after you, who will come from your body; and I will secure his kingdom. It is he who will build a house for me." These things pertain both to the particular and to the general. He exceeds the particular, when he says, "and I will establish his throne for ever." Again pertaining to both: "I will be a father to him, and he will be a son to me. And if there is injustice on his part, I will chastise him with the rod of men and with the strokes of the sons of men. But I will not take my compassion from him as I took it from those whom I removed from my sight; and his house will be secure." Again he exceeds the particular: "and his kingdom will be for ever in my sight, and his throne will be established for ever."[2] And since to promise Christ a throne for ever is evidently to surpass the particular, he is promising the throne to the son of man, and so to the body of Christ, i.e., to the church.[3] For God did not promise on David's account that Christ would reign; Christ "had this glory before the foundation of the world."[4] And, through Isaiah, God addresses Christ in this way: "this will be your greatness, to be called my servant and to establish the tribes of Jacob and to bring scattered Israel back; behold, I have set you as a witness to the people, a light to the nations, to bring salvation to the end of the earth."[5] What is greater for the son of God? To be called his servant and to bring scattered Israel back? Or to be the one through whom Israel itself was made, as well as the heaven and the earth and all things in them, both visible and invisible?[6] Rather he is saying that this greatness belongs to the one, descended from David, who was united to the son of God. For the whole promise to Abraham and to David is this, that their offspring would be united to him from whom are all things and would be his co-heir for ever; it is not that Christ, who was made king of all by the Father, would reign on their account.

---

[1] Jn. 5:24-29

[2] 2 Sam. 7:12-16

[3] Tyconius' thought seems to follow this pattern: the promise of a throne that "will be established for ever" cannot refer to Solomon (who will not live for ever) but must refer to Christ (thus it surpasses the particular); but Christ as son of God has always possessed an eternal throne, and so the promise must be a promise to Christ as son of man who is, of course, identified with his body, the church.

[4] Jn. 17:5, 24

[5] Is. 49:6

[6] The allusion is to Col. 1:16.

Quid dicemus de Salomone? Cum Deo est, an post idolatriam reprobatus est? Si cum Deo dixerimus, impunitatem spondebimus idolorum cultoribus. Non enim dicit Scriptura paenitentiam egisse Salomonem, aut recepisse sapientiam. Si autem reprobatum dixerimus, occurrit vox Dei quae dicit ne terrae quidem regnum Salomoni auferre propter David, sicut scriptum est in Regnorum: *Disrumpens disrumpam regnum tuum de manu tua et dabo eum servo tuo. Verum in diebus tuis non faciam haec propter David patrem tuum; de manu filii tui accipiam eum. Verum omne regnum non accipiam, sceptrum unum dabo filio tuo propter David servum meum, et propter Hierusalem civitatem quam elegi.* Quid enim prodest David, si propter eum filius eius regnum terrae consequeretur caeleste perditurus? Quo manifestum est cum Deo esse Salomonem, cui ne regnum quidem terrae ablatum est propter David, quod et dixerat: *Arguam in virga hominum delicta eius, misericordiam autem meam non auferam ab eo.* Quod si neque reprobatus est neque idolorum cultores regnum Dei possident, manifestum est figuram fuisse Ecclesiae bipertitae Salomonem, cuius *latitudo cordis* et *sapientia sicut harena maris* et idolatria horribilis.

Disrumpens inquit *disrumpam regnum tuum de manu tua, verumtamen in diebus tuis non faciam; de manu filii tui accipiam illud.* Sufficeret *disrumpam,* quid *disrumpens disrumpam?* Aut quomodo *de manu Salomonis,* si dicit *Non faciam in diebus tuis* sed *de manu filii tui accipiam illud?* Iugis operationis est *disrumpens disrumpam,* sicut *Benedicens benedicam et multiplicans multiplicabo semen tuum.* Ostendit enim semper futurum Salomonem in filio, id est in posteris, cuius postumis Salomonis temporibus non auferet Deus regnum sub promissa patrum, sed corrigit illud usque in aeternum et aufert iugiter, secundum idolatriam Salomonis in suo peccato perseverantis. Alias quomodo de manu Salomonis disrumpens disrumpit aut non disrumpit, si non nunc est Salomon in filiis bonus aut malus? Quod autem dicit: *Verum non omne regnum accipio* in speciem redit, incipiens aliam figuram in filio Salomonis et servo.

In Hiesu Nave quoque sic Dominus manifeste in uno homine futurum corpus ostendit, sed hoc loco malum tantummodo. *Peccavit* inquit *populus et transgressus est testamentum quod disposui ad illos, furati sunt de*

What shall we say of Solomon? Is he with God, or was he rejected after his idolatry? If we say he is with God, we will be promising impunity to people who worship idols. For scripture does not say that Solomon did penance or that he regained wisdom. But if we say he was rejected, we are stopped by God's voice saying that, for David's sake, he will not even take away Solomon's earthly kingdom, as it is written in Kings: "tearing, I will tear your kingdom from your hand and will give it to your servant. Yet, for the sake of your father David, I will not do this in your day. I will take it from your son's hand. Nor will I take the whole kingdom. For the sake of David my servant and for the sake of Jerusalem, my chosen city, I will give one scepter to your son."[1] What good is it to David if, for his sake, his son gains the earthly kingdom only to lose the heavenly? It is clear, then, that Solomon is with God; for David's sake, not even his earthly kingdom was taken away, since he had also said: "I will chastise his sins with the rod of man, but I will not take my compassion from him."[2] But if it is neither true that he was rejected nor true that idol-worshipers possess the kingdom of God, then it is manifest that Solomon was a figure of the bipartite church: his "vast heart" and his "wisdom" were "like the sand of the sea,"[3] and his idolatry terrible,

"Tearing," he says, "I will tear your kingdom from your hand; yet I will not do this in your day. I will take it from your son's hand." "I will tear," would be enough. Why does he say, "tearing, I will tear"? And how is it "from Solomon's hand," if he says, "I will not do this in your day," but "will take it from your son's hand"? "Tearing, I will tear," indicates continuous action, like "blessing, I will bless, and multiplying, I will multiply your descendants."[4] For he is showing us that Solomon will always be present in his son, i.e., in his posterity. Under the promises made to the fathers, God does not take away the kingdom of this Solomon in later times, but corrects it for ever—and yet, with respect to the idolatry of the Solomon who perseveres in his sin, he constantly takes it away. How else does he either, tearing, tear or not tear the kingdom from Solomon's hand, if Solomon is not now good or evil as present in his sons? In saying, "nor do I take the whole kingdom," however, he returns to the particular and begins a new figure in Solomon's son and servant.

In Joshua, too, the Lord showed clearly that the body would appear in one person, but in this case only the evil body. "The people have sinned," he said, "and have violated the covenant I established for them. They

---

[1] 1 Kings 11:11-13
[2] 2 Sam. 7:14-15, perhaps conflated with Ps. 89:32-33.
[3] 1 Kings 4:29
[4] Gen. 22:17

anathemate, miserunt in vasa sua, cum solus Achar de tribu Iuda id fecisset. Quod corpus semper futurum intellegens Hiesus sic ait, cum eum occideret: *Exterminet te Deus sicut et hodie.*

Illud etiam multo necessarium est scire, omnes omnino civitates Israhel et gentium uel prouincias, quas Scriptura alloquitur aut in quibus aliquid gestum refert, figuram esse Ecclesiae: aliquas quidem partis malae, aliquas bonae, aliquas vero utriusque. Ergo si sunt aliqua quae etiam in gentes quae foris sunt videantur convenire, in parte tamen quae intus est convenitur omne corpus adversum, sicut in Israhel captivo promittitur gentibus ad Dominum reditus. Impossibile est enim legem loqui ei qui in lege non est; de eo loqui potest, non tamen ad ipsum. Ei si alicubi sine ista occasione nominis Israhel specialiter alienigenas alloquitur, intus omni modo credendi sunt, quoniam, et si eveniebat specialiter quod profetatum est, Ecclesia tamen est. Proprietas denique non omnibus speciebus evenit. Nam et Damascus et Tyrus—quae et Sor— et aliae multae usque nunc extant, quas Dominus penitus tolli nec restaurari dixerat.

In alienigenis autem civitatibus Ecclesiam conveniri apertum est in Ezechiele, cui cum Deus diceret praedicere interitum in Theman, quae est Esau, et in Dagon, quod est idolum Allophylorum, intellexit parabolam esse adversus Hierusalem et templum. *Factus est* inquit *sermo Domini ad me dicens: fili hominis confirma faciem tuam super Theman, respice in Dagon, profetare in silvam summam Nageb, et dices saltui Nageb: audi verbum Domini; haec dicit Dominus, Ecce ego incendo in te ignem, et comedet in te omne lignum viride et omne lignum aridum. Non extinguetur flamma incensa, et comburetur in ea omnis facies in ea a Subsolano usque ad Aquilonem, et cognoscet omnis caro quia ego Dominus succendi illud, non extinguetur ultra. Et dixi: non, Domine. Ipsi dicunt ad me: nonne parabola est haec quae dicitur? Et factus est sermo Domini ad me dicens: propterea fili hominis profetare et confirma faciem tuam ad Hierusalem, respice in sancta eorum, et profetabis super terram Israhel. Haec dicit Dominus, Ecce ego educam gladium meum de vagina sua, et disperdam de te iniquum et iniustum. Sic exiet gladius meus de vagina sua super omnem carnem a Subsolano usque ad Aquilonem, et sciet omnis caro quia ego sum Dominus,*

have stolen what was under ban and put it among their own things."[1]
Yet only Achan, from the tribe of Judah, had done this. Joshua understood that this body would always be present, and so, when he put Achan
to death, he said, "may God destroy you, as he does also today."[2]

It is also very important to know this: that every one of the cities or
provinces of Israel and of the nations that scripture mentions or in
which it reports some event is a figure of the church. Some are figures of
the evil part, some of the good, and some of both. If, therefore, there are
some things which seem also to pertain to the nations on the outside, it is
nevertheless true that the whole enemy body is represented in the part
that is within, just as return to the Lord is promised to the nations in
captive Israel. For it is impossible for the law to speak to someone who
is not under the law; it can speak of him, but not directly to him. Even if
it does somewhere address foreigners on the level of the particular
without using Israel's name, we must not doubt that they are within,
since, even if what was prophesied did occur on the level of the particular, it still refers to the church. Note finally that the specific thing did
not occur in every case of the particular. For Damascus and Tyre—also
called Sor—and many other cities still exist today, even though the Lord
said that they were wholly destroyed and not restored.

It is clear, moreover, that the church is represented in foreign cities
in Ezekiel. When God told Ezekiel to preach destruction to Teman, which
is Esau,[3] and to Dagon, which is the idol of the Allophylites,[4] he understood that this was a parable directed against Jerusalem and the temple.
"The word of the Lord came to me and said: son of man, set your face
against Teman, cast your glance against Dagon, prophesy against the
high woods of the Negeb, and say to the forest land of the Negeb: hear the
word of the Lord: thus says the Lord, behold, I am lighting a fire in you,
and it will burn up every green tree in you and every dry tree. The
burning flame will not go out, and every face will be scorched by it from
the south to the north, and all flesh will know that I, the Lord, kindled
it. It will not be put out again. And I said: no, Lord. They say to me:
what are you saying, is it not a parable? And the word of the Lord came
to me and said: therefore, son of man, prophesy and set your face against
Jerusalem, cast your glance against their sanctuary, and prophesy
against the land of Israel: thus says the Lord: behold, I will draw my
sword from its sheath and will destroy the wicked and the unjust
among you. Thus will my sword leave its sheath against all flesh from
the south to the north, and all flesh will know that I am the Lord, who

---

[1] Josh. 7:11

[2] Josh. 7:29

[3] For Teman and its connection with Esau, see Jer. 49:7-10.

[4] The Allophylites are the Philistines; Tyconius' Latin text has simply
transliterated the name from the Septuagint's Greek.

qui emisi gladium meum de vagina sua, non egredietur ultra. Confirma inquit *faciem tuam super Theman et respice in Dagon,* et interpretatus est dicens: *confirma faciem tuam ad Hierusalem et respice in sancta eorum,* et ostendit non omnem Hierusalem dicens: *disperdam de te iniquum et iniustum,* et ita futurum generaliter ait: *sic exiet gladius meus super omnem carnem a Subsolano usque ad Aquilonem.* Ostendit in Hierusalem esse Theman, quam illic Deus interficiet et Dagon et omnia execrabilia gentium, operante filio David Salomone in filiis suis.   Quae etiam evidenter deiecta templa Dei et demolita atque spiritaliter exusta proiecit in torrentem, id est saeculum, qui nascitur filius David Iosias, ut disrumpatur altare in Bethel, sicut scriptum est: *Altare altare, haec dicit Dominus: ecce filius nascitur domui David, Iosias nomen illi.*

Nineve civitas alienigenarum bipertitae Ecclesiae figura est, sed quia ordine lectionem interpretando persequi longum est, sat erit id quod in speciem convenire non potest dici. *Erat* inquit *Nineve civitas magna Deo,* cum esset adversa Deo, et metropolis Assyriorum quae et Samariam delevit et omnem Iudeam semper oppressit.   Sed in figura Ecclesiae praedicante Iona, id est Christo, omnis omnino liberata est.   Eadem Nineve omnino in sequenti profetia peritura describitur, cui praedicans Dominus *signum* est *Ionae in ventre ceti.* Atque ut et ipse profeta ostendat non esse illam civitatem specialem, interponit aliqua quae speciei modum excedant. *Non erat* inquit *finis gentilibus illius,* cum esset civitas unius gentis. Et iterum: *Multiplicasti mercatus tuos super astra caeli,* id est super Ecclesiam. Et iterum: *Super quem non evenit malitia tua semper?* Numquid potuit unius civitatis malitia super omnem hominem aut semper venisse, nisi illius quam Cain fratris sanguine fundavit *nomine filii sui,* id est posteritatis?

Manifestius adhuc docet profeta Ecclesiam esse Nineve. *Et extendet* inquit *manum suam in Aquilonem*—id est populum solis alienum

sent my sword out from its sheath. It will not return again."[1] He said, "set your face against Teman and cast your glance against Dagon"; and he gave the interpretation when he said, "set your face against Jerusalem and cast your glance against their sanctuary." He also showed that the reference was not to all of Jerusalem when he said, "I will destroy the wicked and the unjust among you"; and he says that this will happen in general: "thus will my sword leave its sheath against all flesh from the south to the north." He shows that Teman is in Jerusalem; and it is there that God will kill Dagon and all the detestable idols of the nations, where David's son Solomon is at work in his sons. Josiah—who is born a son of David in order that the altar in Bethel might be demolished, as it is written: "altar, altar, thus says the Lord: behold a son is born to the house of David, Josiah by name"[2]—also visibly cast these idols into the torrent, i.e., the present world, at a time when the temples of God were cast down, in ruins and spiritually burned up.[3]

The foreign city of Nineveh is a figure of the bipartite church. But because it would take too long to go through the reading and explain it point by point, it will be enough to point out what cannot pertain to the particular. "Nineveh," it says, "was a great city with God,"[4] even though, as the chief city of the Assyrians, it was opposed to God since it destroyed Samaria and constantly oppressed all Judea. But, in a figure of the church, the whole city was completely delivered at the preaching of Jonah, i.e., of Christ. In a subsequent prophecy, the same Nineveh is described as destined to perish completely; in preaching to it, the Lord is "the sign of Jonah in the belly of the whale."[5] And to make sure that the prophet himself also shows that the city is not to be understood on the level of the particular, he introduces some things which exceed the mode of the particular. "There was no end to its peoples," he says, although it was actually a city of one ethnic stock. And again: "you have multiplied your tradings beyond the stars of heaven," i.e., beyond the church. And again: "upon whom has your malice not fallen all the time?"[6] Could the malice of one city have reached everyone or have done so all the time—unless it was the city that Cain founded in his brother's blood and gave "the name of his son,"[7] i.e., his posterity?

The prophet teaches still more clearly that Nineveh is the church. "And," he says, "he will stretch out his hand against the north"—i.e., a people alien to the sun and set in opposition to the south—"and will

---

[1]Ezek. 20:45-21:5

[2]1 Kings 13:2

[3]Tyconius refers to 2 Kings 23:12, 15.

[4]Jon. 3:3

[5]Mt. 12:39, 40

[6]Nahum 3:3, 16, 19

[7]Gen. 4:17

adversum Meridiano—*et perdet Assyrium, et ponet illam Nineve exterminium sine aqua in desertum, et pascentur in medio eius greges, omnes bestiae terrae. Et chameleontes et hericii in laquearibus eius cubabunt, et bestiae vocem dabunt in fossis eius, et corvi in portis eius, quoniam cedrus altitudo eius. Civitas contemnens quae habitat in spe, quae dicit in corde suo Ego sum, et non est post me adhuc! Quomodo facta est in exterminium pascua bestiarum! Omnis qui transit per illam sibilabit, et movebit manus suas. O illustris et redempta civitas, columba quae non audit vocem, non recepit disciplinam. In Domino non est confisa, et ad Deum suum non adpropinquavit, principes eius in ea ut leones frementes, iudices eius ut lupi Arabiae non relinquebant in mane. Profetae eius spiritu elati viri contemptores, sacerdotes eius profanant sacra et conscelerant legem. Dominus autem iustus in medio eius non faciet iniustum.*

Aegyptus item bipertita est. *Ecce* inquit *Dominus sedet super nubem levem et venit in Aegyptum*—nubes corpus est spiritale post baptisma et claritas filii hominis; primus est enim adventus Domini iugiter corpore suo venientis, sicut dicit: *A modo videbitis venientem in nubibus caeli—Et comminuentur manufacta Aegypti a facie illius, et cor ipsorum minorabitur in illis. Et exurgent Aegypti super Aegyptios, et expugnabit homo fratrem suum et homo proximum suum,* et expugnabit *civitas supra civitatem,* et exurget id est Aegyptus super Aegyptum, *et lex supra legem,* sensus scilicet diuersitate sub una lege, *et turbabitur spiritus Aegyptiorum in ipsis, et cogitationes eorum dispargam.* Et postquam nunc generi speciem nunc genus speciei miscuisset adiecit dicens: *Die autem illo erit altare Domini in regione Aegyptiorum, et tituli ad terminos eius Domino. Erit autem in signum in aeternum Domino in regione Aegyptiorum.* Non dixit Decebit esse altare ad terminos Aegypti in aeternum, sed Erit.

Ezechiel vero apertius ostendit totum mundum esse Aegyptum dicens: *O dies! quia prope est dies Domini, dies finis gentium erit. Et veniet gladius super Aegyptios.* Et iungit speciem: *Et erit tumultus in Aethiopia, et cadent vulnerati in Aegypto, et cadent fundamenta eius, Persae et Cretes et Lydii et*

destroy Assyria and make Nineveh a waste, without water, in the desert; and flocks will feed in the midst of her, all the beasts of the earth. And lizards and hedgehogs will sleep in her fancy ceilings, and beasts will give voice in her trenches and ravens in her gates, because she is as lofty as the cedar. A city of disdain, who dwells in hope, who says in her heart: here I am, and there is none after me! How she has gone to ruin, a pasture for the beasts! All who pass through her will hiss and shake their fists. O illustrious and redeemed city, a dove, who did not listen to the call, who did not accept instruction. She did not trust in the Lord and did not draw near to her God. Her rulers were like raging lions; her judges, like Arabian wolves, did not leave in the morning. Her prophets are puffed-up and disdainful men; her priests profane the holy and disgrace the law. But the Lord is just; he will not do injustice in her midst."[1]

Egypt, again, is bipartite. "Behold," he says, "the Lord sits on a swift cloud and comes to Egypt"[2]—the church is the body, spiritual after baptism, and the glory of the son of man; for this is the Lord's first advent, when he comes continuously in his body, as he says, "from this moment you will see him coming on the clouds of heaven"[3]—"and the man-made idols of Egypt will be broken at his presence, and their hearts will shrivel within them. And Egyptians will rise up against Egpytians, and each man will attack his brother and each man his neighbor"; and they will attack, "city against city," and rise up, i.e., Egypt against Egypt, and "law against law"—since, namely, there will be diversities of interpretation under the one law—"and the Egyptians' spirit will be in turmoil within them, and I will scatter their wits."[4] And after mixing now the particular with the general, now the general with the particular, he went on to say: "in that day there will be an altar to the Lord in the land of the Egyptians and pillars to the Lord at its boundaries. And this will be a sign for ever to the Lord in the land of the Egyptians."[5] He did not say, "it will be fitting for there to be an altar at the boundaries of Egypt for ever," but, "there will be."

But Ezekiel shows us more plainly that Egypt represents the whole world when he says: "O the day! For the day of the Lord is near, the day that will be the end for the nations. And the sword will come upon the Egyptians." Then he joins the particular to the general: "and there will be tumult in Ethiopia, and the wounded will fall in Egypt, and her foundations will fall. The Persians and Cretans and Lydians and Libyans

---

[1]Zeph. 2:13-3:5

[2]Is. 19:1

[3]Mt. 26:64. For Tyconius' earlier discussion of this verse and of Christ's two advents, see above, pp. 7-9.

[4]Is. 19:1-3.

[5]Is. 19:19-20

Lybies et omnes commixticii, et filii testamenti mei gladio cadent in ea cum ipsis. Hoc autem factum est, cum post excidium Hierusalem descenderent in Aegyptum et occiderentur illic a Nabuchodonosor secundum Hieremiae profetationem. Fiet autem et generaliter novissimo die, quando cum Aegyptis filii testamenti ceciderunt, Aegyptiorum more viventes.

Item per Ezechielem minatur Deus regi Aegyptiorum et eius multitudini, quod essent terribiles in sanctos, inter incircumcisos deputari, quod non convenit nisi in eos qui sibi circumcisione, id est sacris, blandiuntur. *Quoniam igitur dedit timorem suum super terram vitae, dormiet in medio incircumcisorum cum vulneratis gladio Farao et omnis multitudo eius cum ipso, dicit Dominus.*

Item illic a genere ad speciem: *Haec dicit Dominus, Circumiaciam super te retia populorum multorum, et extraham te in hamo meo, et extendam te super terram. Campi replebuntur tui, et constituam super te omnes aves caeli, et saturabo omnes bestias universae terrae, et dabo carnes tuas super montes, et satiabo sanguine tuo colles, et rigabitur terra ab his quae de te procedunt. A multitudine tua in montibus vepres implebo abs te, et cooperiam caelum cum extingueris, et obscurabo astra eius; solem in nube contegam et luna non lucebit lumen eius. Omnia quae lucent lumen in caelo obscurabuntur super te, et dabo tenebras super terram tuam, dicit Dominus.* Iungit speciem: *Et exasperabo cor populorum multorum, cum ducam captivitatem tuam in nationes in terram quam non noveras.* Excedit speciem: *Et contristabuntur super te multae nationes, et reges earum mentis alienatione stupebunt cum volabit gladius meus super facies eorum in medio eorum, erit ad ruinam suam ex die ruinae tuae.* Redit ad speciem: *Quoniam haec dicit Dominus, Gladius regis Babylonis venit tibi in gladiis gigantum, et deiciam virtutem tuam, pestes a nationibus omnes, et perdent contumeliam Aegypti et conteretur omnis virtus eius.* In genus: *Et perdam omnia pecora eius ab aqua multa, et non turbabit eam pes hominis ultra, et vestigium pecorum non calcabit eam. Tunc requiescent aquae eorum, et flumina eorum ut oleum abibunt, dicit Dominus.* Species: *Et dabo Aegyptum in interitum, et desolabitur terra cum plenitudine sua et dispargam omnes inhabitantes eam.* Genus: *Et scient quia ego sum Dominus.*

and all the motley crowd and the sons of my covenant will fall by the sword with them in her."[1] This, however, did happen, when they went down to Egypt after the fall of Jerusalem and were killed there by Nebuchadnezzar as Jeremiah prophesied. But it will also happen in general at the last day, when the sons of the covenant—the ones living in the manner of the Egyptians—fall with the Egyptians.

Again, through Ezekiel God threatens the king of the Egyptians and his host with being reckoned among the uncircumcised because they had spread terror among the saints, a threat which only applies to people who pride themselves on being within the circumcision, i.e., the sanctuary. "Since he brought terror upon the land of life," therefore "he will lie among the uncircumcised, with those who were cut down by the sword, pharaoh and all his host with him, says the Lord."[2]

There, again, he moves from the general to the particular: "thus says the Lord: I will throw the nets of many peoples over you, and will pull you out with my hook and spread you on the ground. Your fields will be filled; and I will set all the birds of the sky upon you and will fill all the beasts of the whole earth. And I will lay your body on the mountains and glut the hills with your blood; and the earth will be watered with what flows from you. From your host I will fill the briarbushes in the mountains without you, and I will cover the sky when you are extinguished and darken the stars. I will cover the sun with cloud, and the moon will not give its light. All the lights in the heaven will go dark above you, and I will cover your land with darkness, says the Lord." He links the particular to the general: "And I will provoke the heart of many peoples, when I lead you captive among the nations, into a land you do not know." He exceeds the particular: "And many nations will sorrow over you; and their kings will be panic-stricken when my sword speeds over their faces in their midst. Their downfall will hang over them from the day of your downfall." He returns to the particular: "for thus says the Lord: the king of Babylon's sword is coming after you in the swords of his giants; I will bring down your power, all the pestilences from the nations, and they will annihilate the pride of Egypt and all her power will be crushed." He turns to the general: "and I will destroy all her herds by the deep water; and no human foot will soil it again, and no animal footstep strike it. Then their waters will be calm; and their rivers will glide like oil, says the Lord." The particular: "and I will put Egypt to destruction. The land, with all its plenty, will be laid waste; and I will scatter all its inhabitants." The general: "and they will know that I am the Lord."[3]

---

[1] Ezek. 30:2-5

[2] Ezek. 32:32. The threat of being included among the uncircumcised is treated again on p. 135.

[3] Ezek. 32:3-15

Operiam inquit *caelum cum extingueris, et obscurabo astra eius; solem in nube contegam, et luna non lucebit lumen eius. Omnia quae lucent lumen in caelo obscurabuntur super te, et dabo tenebras super terram tuam.* In passione Domini non in terra Aegypti tantum fuerunt tenebrae, sed in toto orbe. Sed nec capta Aegypto obstipuerunt gentes, *expectantes ruinam suam ex die ruinae eius.*

Nam et de Sor scriptum est: *Haec dicit Dominus ad Sor, Nonne a voce ruinae tuae in gemitu vulneratorum, dum interficiuntur gladio in medio tui, commovebuntur insulae? Et descendent a sedibus suis omnes principes maris, et auferent mitras et vestem variam suam despoliabunt se. In stupore mentis stupebunt et timebunt in interitu tuo, et ingemescent super te, et accipient super te lamentationem, et dicent tibi: Quomodo destructa est de mari civitas illa laudabilis, quae dedit timorem suum omnibus inhabitantibus in ea! Et timebunt insulae ex die ruinae tuae.* Iterum de eadem: *In die ruinae tuae ad clamorem vocis tuae gubernatores tui timore timebunt, et descendent de navibus omnes remiges tui, et vectores et proretae maris super terram stabunt, et ululabunt super te voce sua, et clamabunt amarum super te, et imponent super caput suum terram, et cinerem sternent, et accipient super te lamentationem filii eorum, lamentam Sor: Quantum invenisti mercedem de mari! Satiasti gentes multitudine tua, et a commixtione tua locupletasti omnes reges terrae. Nunc autem contrita es in mari, in profundo aquae commixtio tua, et omnis congregatio tua in medio tui. Ceciderunt omnes remiges tui, omnes qui inhabitant insulas contristati sunt super te, et remiges eorum mentis alienatione stupuerunt, et lacrimatus est vultus eorum super te. Mercatores de gentibus exibilabunt te; perditio facta es, et ultra non eris in aeternum, dicit Dominus.* Numquid in unam insulam conveniunt quae dicta sunt, aut sola potuit locupletare omnes reges terrae? Sed aliqua relinquimus locis oportunis, quibus etsi strictim dicantur videri possunt.

Tyrus bipertita est, sicut per Esaiam, qui post multa speciei et generis hoc quoque adiecit dicens: *Erit post septuaginta annos Tyrus sicut canticum fornicariae. Accipe citharam, vagulare, civitas fornicaria oblita; bene citharizare, multa canta, ut tui commemoratio fiat. Et erit post septuaginta annos respectionem faciet Deus Tyri, et iterum restituetur in antiquum, et erit commercium omnibus regnis terrae.* Numquid credibile est universa regna

"I will cover the sky when you are extinguished," he says, "and darken the stars. I will cover the sun with cloud, and the moon will not give its light. All the lights in the heaven will go dark above you, and I will cover your land with darkness."[1] At the Lord's passion, there was darkness not only in the land of Egypt, but in the entire world. Nor were the nations panic-stricken when Egypt was taken captive, "awaiting their downfall from the day of its downfall."

For, of Sor also, it is written: "thus says the Lord to Sor: will not the islands shake at the sound of your downfall, the groaning of the wounded when they are put to the sword in your midst? All the rulers of the sea will get down from their thrones, take off their headbands and strip themselves of their embroidered robes. In a stupor, they will be stunned and terrified at your destruction; and they will moan over you and raise a lament over you and say to you: how that magnificent city has been swept from the sea, the city that brought terror to all its inhabitants! And the islands will be terrified from the day of your downfall."[2] Again, of the same city: "on the day of your downfall, at the clamor of your cry, your helmsmen will be in terror, and all your oarsmen will leave their ships, and the passengers and the pilots will stay ashore. And they will wail over you and cry bitterly over you; and they will put dust on their heads and strew themselves with ashes. And their sons will raise a lament over you, a lament for Sor: what wealth you took from the sea! You satisfied the nations with your abundance, and you made all the kings of the earth rich from your varied store. Now you lie shattered in the sea, your varied store in the depths of the water, and all your company in your midst. All your oarsmen have fallen. All the inhabitants of the islands wept over you, and their oarsmen were panic-stricken and tears covered their faces over you. Traders from the nations will hiss at you; you have gone to ruin and will be no more for ever, says the Lord."[3] Do the things said here apply to a single island, or could one island by itself make all the kings of the earth rich? But we leave some things to their appropriate places, where they can be understood even if mentioned only briefly.

Tyre is bipartite, as in Isaiah who, after saying many things that relate to the particular and to the general, also goes on to say: "after the seventy years Tyre will be like the whore in the song: take your lyre, walk about, forgotten whore, forgotten city. Play your best, sing many songs, to make them remember you. And after the seventy years, God will look again to Tyre; and she will be restored to her former state and will have commerce with all the kingdoms of the earth."[4] Are we to

---

[1] Ezek. 32:7-8
[2] Ezek. 26:15-18
[3] Ezek. 27:27-30, 32-36
[4] Is. 23:15-17

terrarum Tyrum venire negotiandi causa? Quod si veniant, quae utilitas praedixisse futura Tyro *commercia omnibus regnis terrae*, si non Tyrus Ecclesia est in qua orbis terrarum negotium est aeternae vitae? Sequitur enim et ostendit quod sit eius negotium dicens: *Et erit negotiatio eius et merces sancta Domino. Non enim illis colligitur, sed illis qui habitant in conspectu Domini. Omnis negotiatio eius edere et bibere et repleri in signum memoriale in conspectu Domini.* Si ergo negotiatio eius sancta Domini, quomodo potest omnibus esse regnis, nisi ubique fuerit ista Tyrus?

Sequitur enim et aperte ostendit quid sit Tyrus dicens: *Ecce Dominus corrumpet orbem terrarum et vastabit illum et nudabit faciem eius. Disparget eos qui inhabitant in eo, et erit populus sicut sacerdos*—num illius orbis cuius negotiatio sancta Domino?—*et famulus sicut dominus et famula sicut domina. Et erit emens sicut vendens, et qui debet sicut ille cui debetur, et qui fenerat sicut ille qui feneratur. Quia corruptione corrumpetur terra et vastatione vastabitur terra, os enim Domini locutum est ista. Planxit terra, corruptus est orbis terrae, planxerunt alti terrae. Terra autem facinus admisit propter eos quo habitant in ea, quia transierunt legem et mutaverunt iussa, testamentum aeternum. Propterea ergo maledictio comedit terram, quia peccaverunt qui inhabitant in ea. Propter hoc egentes erunt qui inhabitant terram*—numquid illi egentes esse possint, quibus in *omnibus regnis terrae* negotiatio est *edere et bibere et repleri*, non quodam tempore, sed *in signum memoriale in conspectu Domini?*—*et relinquentur homines pauci. Lugebit vitis, lugebit vinum, gement omnes quorum iucundatur anima. Cessavit iucunditas tympanorum, cessavit impudicitia et diuitiae impiorum.* Numquid sanctorum cessabit vox citharae? *Confusi sunt, non biberunt vinum, amarum factum est sicera eis qui bibunt illud. Deserta est omnis civitas, claudent domos ne introeant. Ululate de vino ubique, cessavit omnis iucunditas terrae, et relinquetur civitates desertae, et domus derelictae peribunt. Haec omnia erunt terrae in medio gentium.* Si deserta est omnis civitas, quae sunt gentes in quarum medio ista sunt?

Etsi aliqua horum videntur et iam perspicue fieri, tamen omnia spiritalia sunt. Omnem civitatem desertam spiritaliter mortuam dicit, sed Tyri illius meretricis, non cuius est negotiatio sancta toto orbe. Quod

believe that all the kingdoms of earth will come to Tyre to do business? And if they do come, what is gained by having foretold that Tyre would have "commercial dealings with all the kingdoms of the earth"—unless Tyre is the church, where the world's business is eternal life? For he goes on to show what her business is when he says, "and her business and her profit will be holy to the Lord. For the profit is not taken for themselves, but for those who dwell in the Lord's sight. All her business is to eat and to drink and to be filled as a sign and a memorial in the Lord's sight."[1] If therefore her business is holy to the Lord, how can it deal with all the kingdoms unless this Tyre is everywhere?

For he goes on to show openly what Tyre is, when he says, "behold, the Lord will lay waste the world and make it a desert and scrape its surface bare. He will scatter its inhabitants, priest as well as people"— those belonging to the world whose business is holy to the Lord?— "master as well as slave, mistress as well as maid, seller as well as buyer, creditor as well as debtor, lender as well as borrower. For the earth will be totally laid waste and will be made totally a desert, for the Lord's mouth has declared these things. The earth mourned, the world was laid waste, the depths of the earth mourned. The earth became guilty of crime on account of its inhabitants, because they transgressed the law and altered the precepts, the eternal covenant. Therefore a curse consumes the earth, because its inhabitants sinned. On this account the earth's inhabitants will be in want"—can those be in want whose "business" in "all the kingdoms of the earth" is "to eat and to drink and to be filled," not just for a time, but "as a sign and a memorial in the Lord's sight"?—"and few men will survive. The vine will lament, the wine will lament, all who are glad will sigh. The tambourines' mirth has ended; the shamelessness and the riches of the ungodly have ended." Will the sound of the saints' lyre come to an end? "They have been thrown into confusion; they have not drunk the wine; strong drink has turned bitter to those who drink it. Every city is deserted; they will shut up their houses to keep people out. Wail everywhere about the wine; all merriness has ended on earth; and the deserted cities will remain, and the derelict houses will perish. The earth will suffer all this in the midst of the nations."[2] If "every city is deserted," what are the nations in whose midst these things take place?

Even if some of this seems to be happening now in plain sight,[3] it is still true that these are all spiritual matters. He says that every city is deserted inasmuch as it is spiritually dead; but he means the cities of Tyre the whore, not of the Tyre whose business is holy in all the world.

---

[1] Is. 23:18

[2] Is. 24:1-13

[3] It is impossible to tell what particular events or circumstances, if any, Tyconius may have in mind here.

autem dixit *relinquentur homines pauci*—saluo utique statu—eorum qui peribunt. Pauci relinquuntur ex eis quos spiritaliter mortuos dicit, qui per recordationem vixerint, quos Ecclesia non interfecerit, sicut multis in locis legimus. Sed quia propositum nobis implendum est duobus contenti sumus exemplis. Minatur Deus ignem ex igni Israhel regi Assyriorum, id est adverso corpori, et dicit arsurum uelut stipulam, paucosque ignem fugituros. *Mittet* inquit *Dominus Sabaoth in tuum honorem ignominiam, et in claritatem tuam ignem ardentem, et ardebit lumen Israhel et erit ibi ignis, et sanctificabit illud in flamma ardente*—scilicet *lumen Israhel—et manducabit quasi faenum siluam. In illo die ardebunt montes, et per praeripia fugient, quasi qui fugit a flamma ardenti. Et qui remanserint ab illis erunt numerus, et puer scribet illos. Qui remanserit* inquit *ab illis*, non ab igni, non enim potest ignis qui comburit ardere; qui autem ex combustis superaverint ignis efficientur.

Et in Zacharia legimus illos remanere quos Ecclesia non occiderit, quod ad se convertantur; ceteros vero spiritaliter cruciatibus interficere, si quidem *stantibus* oculos eruat, et *carnes tabescere* faciat. *Habitabit* inquit *in Hierusalem confidens. Et haec erit strages qua caedet Dominus populus, quotquot militaverunt aduersus Hierusalem: tabescent carnes eorum stantibus eis super pedes suos, et oculi eorum fluent a foraminibus eorum, et lingua eorum tabescet in ore eorum. Et erit in illa die alienatio magna super illos, et apprehendet unusquisque manum proximi sui, et implicabitur manus eius manui proximi eius*—id est caecus caecum ducens. *Et Iudas proeliabitur in Hierusalem, et colliget uires omnium populorum, aurum et argentum et uestem in multitudinem nimis. Et haec erit strages equorum et mulorum et camelorum et asinorum et omnium pecorum quae sunt in castris illis, secundum stragem istam. Et erit quicumque relicti fuerint ex omnibus gentibus uenientibus super Hierusalem, et ascendent quotquot annis adorare regem Dominum omnipotentem, celebrare diem festum scenopegiae.*

Aelum alienigenarum est. Huic speciali iungit generalem, monstratque bipertitam. *Haec dicit Dominus, Confringantur arcus in Aelam principatus eorum.* Excedit speciem: *Et superducam quattuor uentos a quattuor cardinibus caeli, et dispergam illos per omnes uentos caeli, nec erit gens quae illuc non ueniat, quae expellat Aelam.* Redit in speciem: *Et*

Moreover, when he said, "few men will survive"—with status unchanged, at any rate—he was speaking of those who will perish. Few survive from those whom he calls spiritually dead, the few who gain life by recollecting themselves, whom the church does not put to death, as we read in many places. But since we must get on with our purpose, we will content ourselves with two examples. God threatens the king of the Assyrians, i.e., the enemy body, with fire from the fire of Israel and says that it will burn like straw and few will escape the flame. "The Lord of hosts," he says, "will send disgrace upon your honor and a burning flame upon your glory; and the light of Israel will take fire, and it will be a fire there; and it will sanctify it in a burning flame"—namely, "the light of Israel"—"and it will consume the forest like dry grass. On that day the mountains will blaze, and they will flee along the riverbanks like one who flees from a burning flame. And their survivors will be few in number, and a child will write them down."[1] "Their survivors," he says—not meaning what survives of the fire, for a fire cannot burn once it consumes its material; those of the burned who survive, however, will become fire.

In Zechariah, too, we read that those remain whom the church does not kill, since they return to themselves; but the rest it spiritually tortures and puts to death, since it plucks out their eyes "while they are still standing" and causes their "flesh to decay." "He will dwell secure," he says, "in Jerusalem. And this is the plague with which the Lord will strike down the peoples, all the peoples that have fought against Jerusalem: their flesh will decay while they are still standing on their feet, and their eyes will flow from their sockets, and their tongues will decay in their mouths. And on that day a great panic will come upon them, and each will grab his neighbor's hand, and his hand will be entwined with his neighbor's hand"—i.e., the blind leading the blind. "And Judah will do battle against Jerusalem, and will gather the forces of all the peoples, gold and silver and clothing in vast quantity. And this will be the plague on the horses and mules and camels and donkeys and all the animals in their camps, like that plague. And there will be some who survive from all the nations that march against Jerusalem; and they will go up each year to worship the king, the Lord the almighty, to celebrate the feast of tabernacles."[2]

Elam is a foreign nation. To Elam, as a particular, he links the general and shows it to be bipartite. "Thus says the Lord: the bows will be broken in Elam, their dominion." He exceeds the particular: "and I will bring four winds from the four points of heaven, and I will scatter them to all the winds of heaven; and there will be no nation which does not come to drive Elam away." He returns to the particular: "and I will

---

[1] Is. 10:16-19
[2] Zech. 14:11-16

terrebo illos coram inimicis eorum qui quaerunt animas eorum, et superducam in eos secundum iram indignationis meae, et mittam post eos gladium meum, donec consumat eos. Iungit genus: *Et ponam sedem meam in Aelam, et perdam inde regem et potentes; eritque in novissimis diebus avertam captivitatem Aelam, dicit Dominus.* Numquid credendum est non fuisse gentem quae non venerit ad expugnandam Aelam, aut illic sedem Domini, cuius captivitatem avertit, nisi Ecclesiae sit figura?

Aliquae uero species sinistrae tantum sunt, ut Sodoma, sicut scriptum est: *Audite verbum Domini principes Sodomorum,* et: *Quae vocatur spiritaliter Sodoma et Aegyptus, ubi et Dominus eorum cruci fixus est.* Ex his Sodomis exiet Loth, quod est, *Discessio,* ut *reveletur homo peccati.*

Babylon civitas adversa Hierusalem totus mundus est, qui in parte sua, quam in hac Hierusalem habet, convenitur. *Visio* inquit *adversus Babyloniam,* et dicit adversum orbem terrarum venturos sanctos Dei milites. *Tollite signum et exaltate vocem illis. Nolite timere exhortamini manus, aperite magistratus, quia ecce ego praecipio. Sanctificati sunt, et voco eos; gigantes veniunt iram meam lenire, gaudentes simul et iniuriam facientes. Vox multarum gentium in montibus similis gentium multarum, vox regum et gentium collectarum,* cum Babylonem gens et rex Medorum everterit. Sequitur enim et dicit qui sunt isti reges, et quae Babylon. *Deus Sabaoth praecepit genti bellatrici venire de longinquo de summo fundamento caeli, Deus et bellatores eius corrumpere universum orbem terrae. Ululate, proximus est enim dies Domini, et contritio a Deo aderit. Propter hoc omnes manus resolventur, et omnis anima hominis trepidabit. Turbabuntur legati, parturitiones enim illos habebunt quasi mulieris parturientis, et patientur circumstantiam; alius ad alium expavescent, et facies eorum sicut flamma commutabuntur. Ecce enim dies Domini insanabilis venit indignationis et irae, ponere orbem terrarum desertum, et peccatores perdere ex eo.* Diem Domini ex quo passus est dicit, ex quo spiritaliter interficitur mundus, interficiente exercitu Dei, dum eius lumen iniqui non vident, sicut sequitur dicens: *Stellae enim caeli et Orion et omnis ornatura caeli lumen non dabunt, et tenebrescet oriente sole lumen et non permanebit lumen eius. Et infligam orbi terrae mala et iniustis peccata eorum, et perdam iniuriam scelestorum et iniuriam superborum humiliabo. Et erunt qui remanserint*—id

terrify them before their enemies, who want to kill them; and I will bring it upon them in my fierce anger and will send my sword after them until it consumes them." He links the general to the particular: "and I will set up my throne in Elam and destroy its king and nobles; but in the last days I will take Elam's captivity away, says the Lord."[1] Are we to believe that every single nation came to do battle against Elam or that the Lord sets up his throne there, among those whose captivity he takes away—unless this is a figure of the church?

Some particulars represent only the left-hand part; for instance, Sodom, as it is written, "hear the word of the Lord, you rulers of Sodom,"[2] and "which is spiritually called Sodom and Egypt, where also their Lord was crucified."[3] From this Sodom Lot will go forth; and that is the "departure" so that "the man of sin may be revealed."[4]

Babylon, as a city set against Jerusalem, is the whole world, which is represented through that part of itself found within this Jerusalem. "A vision," he says, "against Babylon"; and he states that the saints, the soldiers of God, will march against the world. "Raise the standard and sound the cry to them. Have no fear, exhort the troops, show the officers, for, behold, I myself am in command. They have been sanctified, and I call them; giant warriors are coming to relieve my anger, rejoicing even as they wreak havoc. A sound of many nations, a sound of kings and of mustered nations," when the people and king of the Medes overthrew Babylon. For he goes on to say who these kings are and what Babylon is. "The Lord of hosts has commanded a warrior people to come from afar, from the far reaches of heaven, God and his warriors, to lay the whole earth waste. Wail, for the day of the Lord is near, and grief is coming from God. On this account every hand will go limp and every man's heart will tremble. The commanders will be in turmoil, for pains will seize them, like the pains of a woman giving birth; and they will suffer the circumstance. They will terrify each other; and their faces will be changed as if aflame. For, behold, the day of the Lord is coming, inexorable, with fierce anger, to reduce the earth to desert and to purge the sinners from it." He calls it the day of the Lord in that he suffered, in that the world is being killed spiritually, killed by God's army, so long as the wicked do not see the light, as he goes on to say: "for the stars of heaven and Orion and all the ornaments of heaven will give no light, and the light will go dark as the sun rises and its light will not last. And I will punish the world for its evils and the unjust for their sins; and I will destroy the arrogance of the wicked and humble the arrogance of the proud. And those who survive"—i.e., whom the above-

---

[1] Jer. 49:35-39
[2] Is. 1:10
[3] Rev. 11:8
[4] 2 Thess. 2:3

est quos supradicti milites non occiderint—*honorati magis quam aurum quod non tetigit ignem, et homo honoratus erit magis quam lapis ex Sufir. Caelum enim indignabitur et terra commovebitur a fundamentis suis propter animationem irae Domini, in die qua aderit indignatio eius.* Iungit speciem: *Et erit qui relicti sunt quasi capreola fugiens, et sicut ovis errans et non erit qui colligit, ut homo ad populum suum convertatur, et venire in tribum suum festinet. Qui enim inciderit superabitur, et si qui collecti sunt gladio cadent. Et filiae eorum in conspectu eorum cadent, et domos eorum diripient, ex uxores eorum habebunt. Ecce excito vobis Medos, qui non computant pecuniam, neque auro opus est illis.* Subtiliter adstringit genus; cui enim hosti non opus est auro nisi Ecclesiae quae spiritali fruitur vita? *Sagittationes iuvenum confringent, et filiis vestris non miserebuntur, et super nepotes vestros non parcent oculi eorum.*

Omnia spiritaliter, sicut de eadem Babylonia scriptum est: *Felix est qui obtinebit et conlidet parvulos tuos ad petram.* Neque enim regem Medorum quod obtinuerit adversum Babylonem dixit felicem, et non Ecclesiam quae *obtinet et conlidet* filios Babylonis *ad petram* scandali. *Obtinet* autem, sicut scriptum est: *Qui obtinet modo, donec de medio fiat.* Et post multa speciei et generis in clausula periochae aperte ostendit omnes gentes esse Babylonem et eas *in terra* atque *in montibus* suis, id est in Ecclesia, perdere. *Haec dicit Dominus, Ponam Babylonem desertam, ut inhabitent hericii in illa, et erit in nihilum, et ponam illam luti voraginem in perditionem. Haec dicit dominus Sabaoth dicens, Quomodo dixi sic erit, et quomodo cogitavi sic perseverabit, ut perdam Assyrios in terra mea et in montibus meis, et erunt in conculcationem. Et auferetur ab eis iugum eorum, et gloria ab umeris eorum auferetur. Haec cogitatio quam cogitavit Dominus in orbem terrae totum, et haec manus alta super omnes gentes orbis terrae. Deus enim sanctus quod cogitavit quis disparget, et manum illam fortem quis avertet?* Quotienscumque autem post excidium minatur ruinae civitatis

mentioned soldiers do not kill—"will be more honored than gold untouched by fire, each man more honored than a jewel from Ophir. For the heaven will glare and the earth will be shaken from its foundations at the flaring of God's wrath, on the day when his anger comes." He links the particular to the general: "and those who survive will be like a gazelle in flight and like a sheep straying with no one to come after it, each man turning to his own people and hastening to his own tribe. For anyone who attacks will be vanquished and anyone who is captured will fall by the sword. Their daughters will fall before their eyes; and they will plunder their houses and seize their wives. Behold, I stir up against you the Medes, who have no interest in money and no need of gold." Here he subtly ties in the general; for what enemy has no need of gold unless it is the church which finds its enjoyment in spiritual life? "They will break the arrows of your young men, and they will have no mercy on your children; nor will their eyes show pity for your grandchildren."[1]

All this happens spiritually, just as it is written of the same Babylon: "happy is the man who takes and dashes your little children against the rock."[2] For he did not call the king of the Medes happy in that he was going to take Babylon and keep it in check,[3] but rather the church which "takes and dashes" the children of Babylon "against the rock" of the stumbling block.[4] And it "keeps it in check," as it is written: "which now keeps it in check, until it passes from the midst."[5] And after many points relating to the particular and to the general, in a concluding summary he openly shows that Babylon represents all the nations and that he destroys them in his own land and on his own mountains, i.e., in the church. "Thus says the Lord: I will make Babylon a desert, a place where hedgehogs dwell, and it will be reduced to nothingness; and I will make it a swirl of mud to its destruction. Thus says the Lord of hosts: as I have spoken, so will it be, and as I have decided, so will it stand: to destroy the Assyrians in my land and on my mountains, and they will be a thing to trample under foot. And their yoke will be taken from them, and their pride taken from their shoulders. This is the decision which the Lord has taken against the whole world, and this the hand raised against all the nations of the world. For God is holy; and who will dispel what he has decided, and who will turn his mighty hand aside?"[6] Furthermore, whenever he uses the threat that a

---

[1] Is. 13:1-18

[2] Ps. 137:9

[3] I have added this phrase ("and keep it in check") in order to establish the link with 2 Thess. 2:7 which is clearly present in Tyconius' Latin.

[4] The allusion is to 1 Cor. 1:23 and/or Gal. 5:11.

[5] 2 Thess. 2:7

[6] Is. 14:22-27

habitationem bestiarum et avium immundarum, spiritus immundos dicit habitaturos in hominibus quos Spiritus Sanctus deseruerit. Non enim hanc iniuriam possunt interfecti habitatores aut ruina sentire.

Sermones inquit *Amos, quos vidit super Hierusalem;* et coepit: *In tribus impietatibus Damasci et in quattuor non aversabor eam, eo quod secabant serris ferreis in utero habentes.* Et iterum: *In tribus impietatibus Idumaeae et in quatiuor non aversabor eam propter quod persecutus est in gladio fratrem suum.* Et multas alias civitates alienigenarum in Ecclesiae figuram convenit. Ubicumque autem Idumaeam, Theman, Bosor, Seir nominat, fratres malos significat; sunt autem possessiones Esau. *Serras* vero *ferreas* homines dicit duros et asperos, qui secant parturientes Ecclesias.

Item omnes gentes quae sub caelo sunt in civitate Dei iram Dei bibere et illic percuti Hieremias testatur dicens: *Sic dicit Dominus Deus Israhel, Accipe calicem vini meri de manu mea, et potabis omnes gentes ad quas ego mitto te, et voment et insanient a facie gladii, quem ego mitto in medio illarum. Et accepi calicem de manu Domini, et potavi gentes ad quas misit me Dominus ad ipsas: Hierusalem et civitates Iudae et reges eius et principes eius, ut ponerentur in desolationem et in devastationem et in sibilationem; et Farao regem Aegypti et pueros eius et potentes eius et universum populum eius et omnes promiscuos eius; et reges omnes alienigenarum, Ascalonem et Gazam et Accaron et quae contra faciem Azoti; et Idumaeam, et Moabitatem, et filios Ammon, et regem Tyri et regem Sidonis, et reges qui trans mare sunt, et Dedan et Theman et Bosor, et omnem circumtonsam a facie, et omnes promiscuos qui commorantur in deserto, et omnes reges Aelam, et omnes reges Persarum, et universos reges a Subsolano qui longe et qui iuxta sunt, unumquemque ad fratrem suum, et omnia regna terrae quae supra faciem terrae sunt. Et dices illis: Sic dicit Dominus omnipotens, Bibite et inebriamini et vomite, et cadetis et non surgetis a facie gladii, quem ego mitto in medio vestrum. Et erit si noluerint accipere calicem ita ut bibant, dices: Sic dicit Dominus, Bibentes bibetis, quia in civitate in qua invocatum est nomen meum super ipsam incipio vexare vos, et vos purgatione non eritis purgati, quia gladium ego invoco super inhabitantes super terram.*

Potabis inquit *Hierusalem, civitates Iudae et reges eius et principes eius;* deinde dicit: *Et universa regna terrae quae super faciem terrae sunt,* ut ostenderet ab speciali Hierusalem transitum fecisse ad generalem, in qua

ruined city, after its fall, will become a dwelling place for unclean beasts and birds, he is indicating that unclean spirits will take up their dwelling in men who are deserted by the Holy Spirit. For such degradation cannot make any difference to a ruin or to its dead.

"The words of Amos," he says, "which he saw concerning Jerusalem"; and he begins: "for the three offences of Damascus, and the four, I will not relent, because they have cut with iron saws those who are with child." And again: "for the three offences of Edom, and the four, I will not relent, because he persecuted his brother with the sword."[1] And he treats many other foreign cities as figures of the church. Moreover, wherever he names Edom, Teman, Bozrah, Seir, he is signifying the evil brethren; they are Esau's possessions.[2] Indeed his "iron saws" are harsh and savage men who "cut" churches as they are giving birth.

Again, Jeremiah bears witness that all the nations under heaven drink God's wrath in the city of God and are struck down there. He says: "thus says the Lord, the God of Israel: take the cup of unmixed wine from my hand and make all the nations to which I send you drink it; and they will vomit and go mad at the sight of the sword I am sending among them. And I took the cup from the Lord's hand and made the nations to which the Lord sent me drink it: Jerusalem and the cities of Judah and its kings and its rulers, to make them a wasteland and a devastation and an object of hissing; and pharaoh, king of Egypt, and his servants and his nobles and all his people and all his mixed population; and all the foreign kings, Ashkelon and Gaza and Ekron and the land opposite Ashdod; and Edom, and Moab, and the sons of Ammon, and the king of Tyre, and the king of Sidon, and the kings across the sea, and Dedan, and Teman, and Bozrah, and all who wear their hair cut back from the face, and all the mixed population that lives in the desert, and all the kings of Elam, and all the kings of the Persians, and all the kings from the east, far and near, each against his brother, and all the kingdoms on the face of the earth. And you are to say to them: thus says the Lord, the almighty: drink and get drunk and vomit, you will fall and will not get up again at the sight of the sword I am sending among you. And if it turns out that they refuse to take the cup and drink, you are to say: thus says the Lord: you will surely drink, for I am beginning to torment you in the city in which my name is invoked, and you will not be cleansed by the cleansing, for I am summoning a sword against the inhabitants of the earth."[3]

"Make them drink it," he says, "Jerusalem, the cities of Judah and its kings and its rulers"; and finally he says, "and all the kingdoms on the face of the earth," in order to show that he had made the transition

---

[1]Amos 1:1, 3, 11
[2]See Gen. 36:1, 8, 11, 33.
[3]Jer. 25:15-29

sunt omnes gentes terrae quas illic Deus percutiet, sicut et interpretatus est dicens: *Quoniam in civitate in qua invocatum est nomen meum in ipsa incipio vexare vos, et vos purgatione non eritis purgati.* Numquid Hieremias, cum esset in corpore, qui de Iudaea et carcere numquam nisi in Aegyptum tractus, perspicue adiecto mero in calice ut potum dare omnibus gentibus quae sub caelo sunt, aut nunc praeter Ecclesiam profetat? Quodsi tunc quoque et nunc in Ecclesiam locutus est, manifestum est et omnes gentes illicubi Hieremias loquitur convenire in principali eorum parte. Si quid enim summum Satanas in corpore suo, si quid dextrum, si quid grave habet, caelestibus miscuit ut bellantium est mos fortibus fortes opponere. Unde apostolus dicit *non* esse sanctis *pugnam adversum* humana, *sed adversus spiritalia nequitiae in caelestibus.*

V. De temporibus

Temporis quantitas in Scripturis frequenter mystica est tropo synecdoche, aut legitimis numeris, qui multis modis positi sunt et pro loco intellegendi; synecdoche vero est aut a parte totum, aut a toto pars.

Hoc tropo CCCC annos servivit Israhel in Aegypto. Nam dicit Dominus Abrahae: *Sciens scies quia peregrinum erit semen tuum in terra non sua, et dominabuntur eorum et affligent annis CCCC;* Exodi autem Scriptura dicit CCCC XXX annos fuisse Israhel in Aegypto. An non omne tempus servivit? Quaerendum ergo, ex quo tempore: quod invenire facile est. Dicit enim Scriptura non servisse populum, nisi post mortem Ioseph. *Mortuus est* inquit *Ioseph et omnes fratres eius et omnes saeculi illius, filii autem Israhel creverunt et multiplicati sunt et cydaei fuerunt et praevaluerunt nimis, multiplicabat autem eos terra. Exsurrexit autem rex alter super Aegyptum qui ignorabat Ioseph, et dixit genti suae: Ecce gens filiorum Israhel magna multitudo, et valent super nos; venite ergo circumveniamus*

from the particular Jerusalem to the general, in which are included all
the nations of the earth that God will strike down there, as he explained
in saying, "for I am beginning to torment you in the city in which my
name is invoked, and you will not be cleansed by the cleansing." Did
Jeremiah, while he was in the body, ever prophesy outside the church—
a man who was never taken from Judea and his prison except to go to
Egypt, let alone with a visible cup of unmixed wine for him to give to all
the nations under heaven to drink—or does he now prophesy outside the
church? But if, both then and now, he spoke in the church, it is also
manifest that all the nations are represented in their preeminent part in
the place where Jeremiah does speak. For if Satan holds anything of
excellence in his body, anything of the right-hand, anything of
eminence, he mingles it with the heavens, just as it is the custom of
those at war to set the strong against the strong.[1] That is why the apostle
says that the saints' "battle is not against" human powers, "but against
the spiritual hosts of wickedness in the heavens."[2]

V. Times

Temporal quantity, in scripture, often has mystic significance
through the rhetorical figure of synechdoche, or through the specific
numbers involved. The latter are used in a variety of ways and must be
understood according to the context. In synechdoche, however, either a
part represents the whole or a whole represents the part.

It is by this figure that Israel spent 400 years in slavery in Egypt. For
the Lord tells Abraham, "know unmistakably that your descendants will
be exiles in a land not their own; and they will rule over them and
afflict them for 400 years."[3] In Exodus, however, scripture says that
Israel was in Egypt for 430 years.[4] Perhaps they were not in slavery for
the whole time? We need to find out, therefore, when the slavery began;
and this is easy to learn. Scripture reports that the people did not come
into slavery until after Joseph's death. "Joseph died," it says, "and all
his brothers and all of that generation. But the sons of Israel increased
and were multiplied and abounded and grew very strong; the land
teemed with them. Now there arose another king over Egypt who did not
know Joseph; and he said to his people: behold, the people of the sons of
Israel have become a great multitude, and they are stronger than we are.

---

[1] Tyconius' point is that Satan places the "best" of his forces, i.e., the
preeminent part of all the nations, within the church (mingling them "with the
heavens") since that is where the battle between Christ's body and the enemy
body is most fierce and most subtle and thus where the strong are most needed to
oppose the strong.

[2] Eph. 6:12

[3] Gen. 15:13

[4] See Ex. 12:40.

eos. Si autem post mortem Ioseph coepit servire populus, ex CCCC et XXX annis, quibus in Aegypto moratus est, deducimus LXXX annos regni Ioseph—regnavit autem a XXX annis usque in CX—et erunt reliqui servitutis Israhel anni CCCL, quos Deus dixit CCCC. Si autem omni tempore peregrinationis suae servivit Israhel, plus est quam Deus dixit; si ex morte Ioseph secundum Scripturae sanctae fidem, minus est. Quo manifestum est centum a toto partem esse, nam post CCC annos pars aliorum centum anni sunt: propterea dixit CCCC annos.

Sic in omni summa temporis, ut puta post novem dies prima hora decimi diei dies est, aut post novem menses primus dies mensis est, sicut scriptum est: *In utero matris figuratus sum caro decem mensuum tempore coagulatus in sanguine.* Sicut autem in prima parte cuiusque temporis totum tempus est, ita et novissima hora totus dies est, aut reliquiae mille annorum mille anni sunt. Sex dies sunt mundi aetas, id est sex milia annorum. In reliquiis sexti diei, id est M annorum, natus est Dominus, passus et resurrexit. Itidem reliquiae M annorum dictae sunt mille anni primae resurrectionis. Sicut enim reliquiae sextae feriae, id est tres horae, totus dies est, unus ex tribus sepulturae Domini, ita reliquiae sexti diei maioris quo surrexit Ecclesia totus dies est, id est M anni.

Hoc enim tropo constat *tres dies et tres noctes.* Noctis autem et diei XXIIII horae unus dies est, nec adiciuntur noctes diebus nisi certa ratione. Alias dies solos dicimus, sicut Apostolus dicit mansisse apud Petrum diebus XV: numquid opus erat dicere totidem et noctibus? Sic enim scriptum est: *Vespera et mane dies unus.* Quod si nox et dies unus dies est, novissima hora diei et totum diem et noctem transactam retinet. Similiter et novissima hora noctis totam noctem et diem futuram: hora enim pars est utriusque temporis. Hora qua sepultus est Dominus pars est sextae feriae cum sua nocte quae transierat, et hora noctis in qua

Come, therefore, we must oppress them."[1] Now if the people's slavery began after Joseph's death, then we subtract the 80 years of Joseph's reign—he reigned from the age of 30 to the age of 110[2]—from the 430 years of their stay in Egypt; and there remain, for Israel's slavery, 350 years— which God called 400. Now if Israel was in slavery for the whole time of its exile, then that is more than God said; if only after Joseph's death, in accord with the reliability of holy scripture, then that is less. From this, it is plain that the hundred is a whole representing a part; for the years following the first 300 years are part of another hundred, and that is why he spoke of 400 years.

So also in the case of every temporal sum: for example, after nine days the first hour of the tenth day is reckoned as a day or, after nine months, the first day is reckoned as a month (as it is written: "in my mother's womb I was fashioned as flesh, made firm in her blood during a period of ten months"[3]). Moreover, just as the whole time is reckoned in the first part of any time period, so also the last hour is reckoned as a whole day, or what is left of a thousand years is reckoned as a thousand years. The world's age is six days, i.e., six thousand years. In what is left of the sixth day, i.e., of these 1000 years, the Lord was born, suffered and rose again. Similarly what is left of the 1000 years is called the thousand years of the first resurrection. For just as what was left of the sixth day of the week, i.e., three hours, is reckoned as a whole day—one of the three that the Lord was in the tomb—so what is left of the greater sixth day on which the church rose from the dead is reckoned as a whole day, i.e., 1000 years.

For it is by this figure that the "three days and three nights"[4] are determined. Now the 24 hours of a night and a day are reckoned as one day; and the nights are not mentioned in addition to the days unless there is some special reason. Otherwise we speak only of the days, as when the apostle says that he stayed with Peter for 15 days.[5] Was there any need for him to add that he had also stayed as many nights? For so it is written: "evening and morning, one day."[6] But if a night and a day are reckoned as one day, then the last hour of the day represents both the whole day and the preceding night. And similarly the last hour of the night represents the whole night and the upcoming day; for that hour is a part of both time periods. The hour at which the Lord was placed in the tomb is part of the sixth day of the week together with the previous night; and the hour of the night at which he rose again is a part of the

---

[1]Ex. 1:6-10
[2]See Gen. 41:46 and Gen. 50:22.
[3]Wisd. 7:1-2
[4]Mt. 12:40
[5]See Gal. 1:18.
[6]Gen. 1:5

resurrexit pars est imminentis diei. Ceterum si neque in die praesenti nox est praeterita neque in nocte praesenti dies crastinus, non die resurrexit Dominus sed nocte. Quoniam dies ab ortu solis est, sicut scriptum est: *Luminare maius initium diei*; Dominus autem ante solis ortum resurrexit. Nam Marcus dicit: *Oriente sole,* non orto sed *oriente,* id est ad ortum eunte; Lucas autem: *Diluculo.* Sed ne de hac locutione ambigeretur alteri euangelistae aperte noctem fuisse testantur. Nam Matheus nocte dicit venisse mulieres ad monumentum et vidisse Dominum, Iohannes vero *cum adhuc tenebrae essent.* Si autem Dominus ante solem, id est ante initium diei resurrexit, nox illa pars est illucescentis diei. Quod et competit operibus Dei, ut non dies obscuretur in noctem sed nox lucescat in diem. Ipsa enim nox illuminatur et efficitur dies, quod est figura eorum quae facturus erat in Christo, *quoniam Deus qui dixit de tenebris lumen fulgere fulsit in cordibus nostris,* qui illuminavit tenebras, sicut scriptum est: *Tenebrae tuae sicut meridies erunt,* et: *Nox transivit, dies autem adpropinquavit; sicut in die decenter ambulemus.* Prius est enim quod carnale est, *deinde quod spiritale.*

Dies ergo primus et novissimus a toto pars est. Solus medius plenus fuit a vespera in vesperam secundum Dei conditionem atque praeceptum, sicut Mosi dicit in Levitico *a vespera in vesperam* observari diem sabbatorum. Quidam autem putant ex die computandum, quoniam Dominus tres dies et noctes dixit, non tres noctes et dies. Sed hoc non longa ratione destruitur. Si enim ex die initium sepulturae, in nocte finis; si autem in die finita est, a nocte coepit. Nam si dies utrimque concluditur, plus erit unus dies. Dicunt praeterea non posse in die noctem esse praeteritam nec in nocte diem futurum, sed separatos tres dies et noctes oportere adsignari, computantes primum diem quo cruci fixus est, alterum trium horarum separatarum, tertium sabbati—erit

upcoming day. For the rest, if we are neither to reckon "last night" in the present day nor to reckon "tomorrow" in the present night, then the Lord rose again at night and not during the day. For the day is reckoned from the sun's rise, as it is written: "the greater light to begin the day."[1] But the Lord rose before sunrise. For Mark says, "as the sun was rising,"[2] not "had risen" but "was rising," i.e., was approaching sunrise. And Luke has, "at dawn."[3]   But, lest any ambiguity arise from this expression, the other evangelists plainly testify that it was night. Matthew says that the women came to the tomb by night and saw the Lord;[4] and John has, "while it was still dark."[5] Now if the Lord rose before the sun came up, i.e., before the day began, then that night is a part of the dawning day. And this befits God's works, that day should not be darkened into night but night be lightened into day. For the very night is illumined and becomes day, which is a figure of the things he was going to do in Christ, "for the God who told the light to shine out of darkness has shone in our hearts,"[6] the God who illumined the darkness, as it is written: "your darkness will be like midday,"[7] and: "the night has passed, day is at hand; let us live decently, as in the day."[8] For first comes what is carnal, "then what is spiritual."[9]

The first day and the last, therefore, are parts representing the whole. Only the middle day was a full day, running from one evening to the next, in keeping with God's stipulation and precept, as he tells Moses in Leviticus that the sabbath day is to be observed "from one evening to the next."[10] Now some people imagine that the reckoning ought to begin with a day, since the Lord said, "three days and nights," not "three nights and days." But this notion is overturned by a consideration that is not far to seek. If the time in the tomb began on a day, it ended on a night; or if it ended on a day, it began on a night. For if the argument is that it both began and ended by day, there will be one day too many. Furthermore, they claim that the previous night cannot be reckoned in the day nor the upcoming day in the night. Rather we must account for three separate days and nights, counting the day he was crucified as the first, the three separated hours as the second, the sabbath as the third—and the

---

[1]Gen. 1:16
[2]Mk. 16:2
[3]Lk. 24:1
[4]See Mt. 28:1.
[5]Jn. 20:1
[6]2 Cor. 4:6
[7]Is. 58:10
[8]Rom 13:12, 13
[9]1 Cor. 15:46
[10]Lev. 23:32

dominicus dies quartus! Qui autem hanc circumventionem vitant consentiunt a nocte quidem computandum, sed noctes a diebus debere separari, dicentes in tribus horis tenebrarum importunarum primam noctem, alteram sabbati, tertiam illucescentis dominici. Noctes quidem veluti tres sunt, sed dies duo: primus in tribus horis post tenebras, secundus sabbati! Non enim qui separatos dies promittit potest dicere in nocte qua resurrexit fuisse diem futurum. Quod si in id consensit, consentiat necesse est in reliquis diei sextae feriae fuisse noctem praeteritam. Quasi tenebrae importunae fuerunt, tres tamen horae lucis eiusdem sunt diei, nec amiserunt ordinem suum, quo minus pars esset diei ac noctis suae. Taceo tres horas tenebrarum noctem esse non potuisse, quod praeter ordinem fuerint conditionis Dei. Quicquid enim signi est non turbat elementorum rationalem cursum. Non enim quia stetit sol et luna in diebus Hiesu et Ezechiae solus sol reversus est; aliquid cursus inter solem et lunam mutilatum est et detractum vel additum diei ac nocti, et nova exinde coepit temporum aut neomeniae supputatio, quam statuit Deus in sole et luna esse *in tempora dies et annos*, sicut in Genesi scriptum est. Multo magis in illo die nihil turbatum est, cui non sunt adiectae tres horae tenebrarum ut essent XV horarum, sed pars ipsius diei obscurata est—sexta in nonam. Quod si non solem obscuratum et rursum ostensum diem dicimus, quod nomen, quem ordinem damus ipsi diei qui fuisse dicitur inter sextam feriam et sabbatum, nisi bis sabbatum fuit et ebdomadas illa octo dies habuit? Certe, si contentio ratione minime sedari potest, compendio probamus tres horas tenebrarum non pertinere ad sepulturam Domini, eo quod adhuc viveret. Non enim potuit esse *in corde terrae* nisi ex quo mortuus est et sepultus est, quod factum est in tribus horis sextae feriae intra duodecimam. Quoniam post occasum solis non licebat Iudaeis sepelire, cum esset cena pura initium sabbati, sicut Iohannes dicit: *Illic ergo propter cenam puram Iudaeorum, quoniam*

Lord's day as the fourth! Those who want to avoid this fraudulent reasoning agree that the reckoning must begin with a night, but claim that the nights ought to be kept distinct from the days. They maintain that the first night comes in the three hours of unaccustomed darkness, the second in the night of the sabbath, the third in the night of the dawning Lord's day. And indeed there are three "nights" here, but only two days: the first in the three hours following the darkness, the second in the sabbath! For no one who pledges to keep the days distinct from the nights can say that the upcoming day is reckoned in the night on which Christ rose again. But if he has agreed to this, let him also agree that the previous night must have been reckoned in what was left of the sixth day of the week. And although[1] the darkness was unusual, the three hours of light still belong to the same day; nor did they come out of their proper order so as to be any less a part of the day and its night. I pass over the fact that the three hours of darkness could not have been a night because they would then have fallen outside the order of God's creation. For no sign upsets the rational course of the elements. From the fact that the sun and the moon stood still in Joshua's day[2] or that the sun alone reversed its course in Hezekiah's time,[3] it does not follow that any part of the round between sun and moon was crippled or that anything was subtracted from or added to the day and the night. No new computation of times or of the new moon began at those points, other than the one God established in the sun and the moon to be "for times, days and years,"[4] as it is written in Genesis. All the more, then, is it true that nothing was disturbed on that day. Three hours of darkness were not added to it so as to make a total of 15 hours; rather a part of the day itself was darkened from the sixth hour to the ninth. And if we do not call it day when the sun darkened and then showed itself again, what name, what place, are we to give to this day which is said to have fallen between the sixth day and the sabbath—except to say that it was a second sabbath and that that week had eight days? Surely, at least if the dispute can be stilled by reason, we can prove in a very few words that the three hours of darkness have nothing to do with the Lord's time in the tomb. For the fact is that he was still alive. He could not be "in the heart of the earth"[5] until after he had died and was buried, and that happened in the final three hours of the sixth day preceding the twelfth hour. For Jews were not permitted to bury the dead after sunset, since the sabbath began with a pure meal, as John says: "therefore, because of the pure meal of the Jews

---

[1]Here I depart from Burkitt's text, reading *quae si* rather than *quasi*.

[2]See Josh. 10:12-14.

[3]See 2 Kings 20:8-11.

[4]Gen. 1:14

[5]Mt. 12:40

proximum erat monumentum, posuerunt Iesum. Dies autem noctibus dignitate non novitatis ordine praeferuntur, ut omnes masculi primogenitis, sicut dictum est: *Genuit filios et filias et obiit,* cum contra legem sit naturae ut omnes illi masculos primum genuisset. Nobis autem totum tempus dies est; omnia nova sunt, figurae transierunt.

Ex legitimis numeris sunt septenarius, denarius, duodenarius. Idem autem est numerus et cum multiplicatur, ut LXX, DCC; vel totiens in se, ut septies septeni uel decies deni. Sed aut perfectionem significant, aut a parte totum, aut simplicem summam. Perfectionem, ut VII spiritus Ecclesiae, aut ut dicit: *Septies in die laudabo te,* aut: *Septies tantum recipiet in isto saeculo.* Similiter decies, ut alius evangelista dicit: *Centies tantum recipiet in isto saeculo.* Et Danihel angelorum et caeli vel Ecclesiae innumerabilem multitudinem denario numero complexus est dicens: *Milies milia apparebant illi et decies milies decies milia circumsistebant.* Et David *Currus* inquit *Dei decies milies tantum.* Et de omni tempore David: *In mille saecula.* Item per duodenarium de omni Ecclesia dictum est CXLIIII. Et duodecim tribus omnes gentes, sicut: *Iudicabitis XII tribus Israhel.* A parte totum est, quoniam certum tempus legitimis numeris definitur ut in Apocalypsi: *Habebitis pressuram X dies,* cum significet usque in finem. LXX autem annos in Babylone idem tempus esse importunum est nunc probare.

and since the tomb was close by, they laid Jesus there."[1] Furthermore, days take precedence over nights as a matter of worth, not by being first in order, just as all male children take precedence over firstborn children (as it is said, "he had sons and daughters, and he died,"[2] even though it runs against nature's law that he should have had all the male children first). For us, however, the whole time is day; all things are new, the figures have passed away.

Among the specific numbers there are the number seven, the number ten and the number twelve. Moreover the number has the same significance even when it is multiplied, 70 or 700 for example, or when it is squared, seven times seven or ten times ten for example. But they signify either a perfect whole or a part representing a whole or a simple sum. Examples of a perfect whole are the 7 spirits of the church[3] or when he says, "seven times a day will I praise you,"[4] or "he will receive seven times as much in this age."[5] Likewise ten times, as another evangelist says, "he will receive a hundred times as much in this age."[6] Daniel also encompassed the innumerable host of the angels, whether of heaven or of the church, with the number ten when he said, "a thousand thousands were serving him and ten thousand times ten thousand were standing round him."[7] And David said, "God's chariots, ten thousand times as many."[8] And David, referring to all time: "for a thousand ages."[9] Again, through the number twelve, 144,000 is mentioned with reference to the whole church.[10] And all the nations are indicated in the twelve tribes; for example, "you will judge the 12 tribes of Israel."[11] It is a case of a part representing a whole that a fixed period of time is defined with specific numbers, as in the Apocalypse. "you will have tribulation for 10 days,"[12] even though it means to the end of time. This is not the moment, however, to show that the 70 years in Babylon have the same temporal reference.

---

[1] Jn. 19:42
[2] Gen. 5:4, 5
[3] See Rev. 1:4.
[4] Ps. 119:164
[5] Lk. 18:30
[6] Mk. 10:30
[7] Dan. 7:10
[8] Ps. 68:17
[9] Ps. 105:8
[10] See Rev. 7:4.
[11] Mt. 19:28
[12] Rev. 2:10

Praeter legitimos etiam numeros, quodcumque tempus in quodcumque numero frequenter breviavit Scriptura, sicut supradictum tempus Hora appelatum est, dicente apostolo: *Novissima hora est;* et Dies, sicut: *Esse nunc dies salvationis;* et Annus, sicut per Esaiam: *Praedicare annum Domini acceptabilem.* Quoniam non ille quo Dominus praedicavit solus fuit acceptabilem, sed et iste quo praedicat, sicut dictum est: *Tempore accepto exaudivi te,* quod apostolus interpretatur: *Ecce nunc tempus acceptabile.* Finis denique huius anni diem iudicii iunxit dicens: *Praedicare annum acceptabilem et diem retributionis.* Et David *Benedices* inquit *coronam anni bonitatis tuae.*

Aliquando hora dies et mensis annus est, sicut in Apocalypsi: *Parati in horam et diem et mensem et in annum,* quod est tres anni et dimidius. Ibidem, menses pro annis: *Datum est ei laedere homines mensibus quinque.* Aliquando dies denario numero C dies sunt, sicut in Apocalypsi: *Dies M CCLX,* nam milies ducenties centies et sexagies centeni centumviginti sex milia dies sunt, qui fiunt anni CCCL mensibus tricenorum dierum. Ibidem, unus mensis denario numero centum menses sunt, ut: *Civitatem sanctam calcabunt mensibus XLII,* nam XLII centeni IIII et CC menses sunt, qui sunt anni CCCL.

Tempus aut annus est aut centum anni, sicut *Tempus et tempora et dimidium temporis,* quod est aut tres anni et dimidius aut CCCL. Item unus dies aliquando centum anni sunt, sicut de Ecclesia scriptum est iacere *in civitate ubi et Dominus* eius *cruci fixus est tres dies et dimidium,* et: *Oportet filium hominis Hierusalem ire, et multa pati a senioribus et principibus*

Beyond the specific numbers, scripture also has often abbreviated a given time with a given number. The above mentioned time,[1] for instance, was called an hour, as when the apostle said, "it is the last hour,"[2] and a day, as in "behold, now is the day of salvation,"[3] and a year, as in Isaiah, "to proclaim the acceptable year of the Lord."[4] For not only was the year in which the Lord preached acceptable, but also the year in which he preaches—as it is said, "at the accepted time, I heard you,"[5] which the apostle explains: "behold, now is the acceptable time."[6] Note finally that he linked the day of judgment to the end of this year when he said, "to proclaim the acceptable year and the day of retribution."[7] And David said: "you will bless the crown of the year of your goodness."[8]

Sometimes hour, day and month each represent a year, as in the Apocalypse: "held ready for an hour and a day and a month and for a year,"[9] which represents three and a half years. In the same passage, months stand for years: "it was allowed to hurt men for five months."[10] Sometimes, in virtue of the number ten, a day represents 100 days, as in the Apocalyse: "1260 days."[11] For one thousand two hundred and sixty times one hundred equals one hundred twenty-six thousand days, which makes 350 years with months of thirty days each. In the same place, by the number ten, one month represents a hundred months, as in: "they will trample on the holy city for 42 months."[12] For 42 hundreds equals 4200 months, which makes 350 years.

A time is either a year or a hundred years, as in "for a time and times and half a time,"[13] which is either three and a half years or 350 years. Likewise one day sometimes represents a hundred years, as when it is written of the church that, "for three and a half days," it will be left for dead "in the city where" its "Lord, too, was crucified,"[14] and that "the son of man must go to Jerusalem, and suffer many things at the

---

[1]That is, the period from the present to the end of time.

[2]1 Jn. 2:18

[3]2 Cor. 6:2

[4]Is. 61:2 as cited in Lk. 4:19.

[5]Is. 49:8 as cited in 2 Cor. 6:2.

[6]2 Cor. 6:2

[7]Is. 61:2 as cited in Lk. 4:19.

[8]Ps. 65:11

[9]Rev. 9:15

[10]Rev. 9:10

[11]Rev. 11:3

[12]Rev. 11:2

[13]Rev 12:14

[14]Rev. 11:8, 9

sacerdotum et scribis, et occidi, et post tres dies resurgere; ipse enim tertio surrexit.

Generatio aliquotiens et C anni sunt, sicut Dominus dicit Abrahae: *Quarta autem generatione revertentur huc.* In Exodo vero non de servitutis sed de totius peregrinationis tempore dictum est: *Quinta autem generatione ascendit* populus *ex Aegypto,* id est post CCCC et XXX annos. Item generatio aliquotiens X anni sunt, sicut Hieremias dicit: *Eritis in Babylonia usque ad generationes VII.*

Ternarium numerum eundem esse, qui et denarius—id est plenus—in Euangeliis deprehenditur. Nam Matheus dicit tribus servis creditam Domini substantiam; Lucas vero X, quos X in tres redigit, dum et ipse a tribus dicit exactam rationem.

Aliquotiens unus dies M anni sunt, sicut scriptum est: *Qua die gustaveritis ex arbore morte moriemini.* Et VII dies primi VII anni sunt; sex diebus operatus est Dominus *et requievit ab omnibus operibus suis die septimo, et benedixit et sanctificavit illum.* Dominus autem dicit: *Pater meus usque nunc operatur.* Sicut enim mundum istum sex diebus operatus est, ita mundum spiritalem, qui est Ecclesia, per sex milia annos operatur, cessaturus die septimo quem benedixit, fecitque aeternum.

Hoc est quod Dominus inter cetera mandata nihil aliud crebrius praecepit, quam ut observemus et diligamus diem sabbatorum. Qui autem praecepta Dei facit sabbatum Dei diligit, id est septimum diem quietis aeternae. Propterea Deus hortatur populum non intrare portas Hierusalem cum onere in die sabbati, et minatur portis et intrantibus per eas et exeuntibus, sicut Hieremiae mandat dicens: *Vade sta in portis filiorum populi tui, in quas ingrediuntur reges Iuda et egrediuntur, et in omnibus portis Hierusalem, et dices ad eos: Audite verbum Domini qui intratis in portas istas. Haec dicit Dominus, Custodite animas vestras, et nolite tollere onera in die sabbatorum et nolite exire portas Hierusalem et nolite effere onera de domibus vestris in die sabbatorum, sicut mandavi*

hands of the elders and the chief priests and the scribes, and be killed, and rise again after three days";[1] for the Lord himself arose on the third day.

A generation, too, often represents 100 years, as when the Lord says to Abraham, "in the fourth generation they will come back here."[2] And in Exodus with reference not to the period of slavery but to the whole time of exile, it is said, "and in the fifth generation," the people "went up from Egypt,"[3] i.e., after 430 years. Likewise a generation often represents 10 years, as when Jeremiah says, "you will be in Babylon for as long as 7 generations."[4]

In the gospels one grasps that the number three represents the same as the number ten—i.e., what is complete. For Matthew says that a master's property was entrusted to three servants, but Luke to 10—which 10 he reduces to three when he also says that a reckoning was required from three servants.[5]

Often one day represents 1000 years, as when it is written: "on the day you eat from the tree, you will surely die."[6] And the first seven days represent 7000 years; the Lord worked for six days "and on the seventh day he rested from all his works, and he blessed that day and made it holy."[7] Yet the Lord says, "my father is working even until now."[8] For just as he made that world in six days, so he makes the spiritual world, which is the church, in the course of six thousand years; and he will stop on the seventh day, which he has blessed and has made eternal.

This is why the Lord prescribed no command more often than that we should keep and love the sabbath day. Now the person who does God's commands is the person who loves God's sabbath, i.e., the seventh day of eternal rest. It is on this account that the Lord exhorts the people not to enter the gates of Jerusalem with any burden on the sabbath day and threatens the gates, as well as those who enter and leave through them. Thus he commands Jeremiah: "go, stand at the gates of the sons of your people, through which the kings of Judah come in and go out, and at all the gates of Jerusalem; and say to them: hear the word of the Lord, you who enter through these gates. Thus says the Lord: take heed for yourselves and carry no burdens on the sabbath day, do not go out through the gates of Jerusalem and take no burden from your houses on the sabbath day, just as I commanded your fathers. And they did not

---

[1]Mt. 16:21

[2]Gen. 15:16

[3]Ex. 13:18 (cf. Septuagint)

[4]Baruch 6:2 (cf. Vulgate)

[5]See Mt. 25:14-15 and Lk. 19:13-26.

[6]Gen. 2:17

[7]Gen. 2:2, 3

[8]Jn. 5:17

patribus vestris; et non audierunt in auribus suis, et induraverunt cervicem suam super patres suos, ut me non audirent neque percipirent disciplinam. Eritque si me audieritis, dicit Dominus, ut non inferatis onera per portas civitatis huius in die sabbatorum, ut non faciatis omne opus vestrum, et sanctificetis diem sabbatorum, et intrabunt per portas civitatis huius reges et principes sedentes in sede David et ascendentes in currus et equos, ipsi et principes eorum, viri Iuda et qui inhabitant Hierusalem. Et habitabitur *civitas haec in aeternum, et venient de civitatibus Iuda et civitatibus Hierusalem, et de terra Benjamin et de terra campestri et de terra quae ad Austrum, afferentes holocausta et incensa et manna et tus, ferentes laudationem in domum Domini. Et si me non audieritis ut sanctificetis diem sabbatorum, ut non portetis onera neque intretis per portas Hierusalem in die sabbatorum, et succendam ignem in portis eius, et consumet itinera Hierusalem et non extinguetur.* Sufficeret breviter mandasse non operari sabbatis; ut quid *Nolite inferre onera per portas Hierusalem?* Aut si opus erat et operis speciem dicere, quid *Nolite inferre per portas?* Non enim aliqui per muros et tecta infert onera in civitatem.

Hierusalem bipertita est, et portae eius bipertitae. Per portas inferorum exitur de Hierusalem sancta, et per easdem intratur in maledicta. Qui autem per portas intrant caeli intrant in aeternam Hierusalem, ut *reges in curribus et in equis sedentes in sede David,* sicut per Esaiam: *Adducent fratres vestros ex omnibus gentibus donum Domino cum equis et curribus in splendore mulorum cum umbraculis in sanctam civitatem.* Sanctae portae civitatis Hierusalem Christus est, et vicarii eius custodes legis, *interficientes* vero *prophetas et lapidantes missos ad se.* Porta diabolus est, et vicarii eius pseudoapostoli praedicatores legis, *claves regni caelorum* alto sensu abscondentes. Ipsi sunt *portae* quae *non vincunt Ecclesiam,* quae *supra petram fundata est,* quoniam *firmum fundamentum*

listen at all; and they stiffened their necks against their fathers, neither listening to me nor accepting instruction. If you listen to me, says the Lord, and bring no burdens in through the gates of this city on the sabbath day and do none of your work and keep the sabbath day holy, this is how it will be: through the gates of this city will enter kings and princes occupying the throne of David and going up in chariots and on horses, they and their princes, the men of Judah and the inhabitants of Jerusalem. And this city will be inhabited for ever; and they will come from the cities of Judah and the cities of Jerusalem and from the land of Benjamin and from the plainsland and from the land to the south, bringing whole offerings and incense and manna and frankincense, bringing praises to the house of the Lord. But if you do not listen to me and do not keep the sabbath day holy and carry burdens and enter through the gates of Jerusalem on the sabbath day, then I will light a fire in its gates, and it will devour the streets of Jerusalem, and it will not be quenched."[1] A brief command not to work on the sabbath would have been enough; why add, "bring no burdens in through the gates of Jerusalem"? Or, if there was reason to mention the specific kind of work as well, why add, "in through the gates"? No one brings burdens into a city through the walls or the roofs.

Jerusalem is bipartite; and its gates are bipartite. Through the gates of the underworld one leaves the holy Jerusalem; and through the same gates one enters the accursed places. But those who enter through the gates of heaven enter the eternal Jerusalem like "kings in chariots and on horses, occupying the throne of David,"[2] as it says in Isaiah: "they will bring your brothers from all the nations to the holy city, with horses and chariots in a splendor of mules with sunshades, an offering to the Lord."[3] The holy gates of the city of Jerusalem are Christ; and his representatives are the keepers of the law, who assuredly "kill the prophets and stone those who are sent to them."[4] The gate is the devil; and his representatives are false apostles, preachers of the law who hide "the keys of the kingdom of heaven"[5] with its deeper meaning. These are "the gates" which "do not prevail against the church,"[6] which "was built on rock";[7] for "God's foundation stands firm," as it is written: "the

---

[1]Jer. 17:19-27

[2]Jer. 17:25

[3]Is. 66:20

[4]Mt. 23:37. This negative characterization of Christ's representatives is a bit odd since it seems to run counter to the antithesis between Christ and the devil developed here. Perhaps it is a tacit reference to the Donatist bishops who opposed Tyconius.

[5]Mt. 16:19 with an allusion, perhaps, to Mt. 23:13.

[6]Mt. 16:18

[7]Mt. 7:25

Dei stat, sicut scriptum est: *Cognovit Dominus qui sunt eius.* Si quis autem per praecepta praesidentium *cathedrae Mosi* introiit, per Christum intrat—ipsius enim sunt praecepta, ipse exponit onus peccatorum suorum—et sine illo intrat in requiem sabbati. Si quis vero non per praecepta sed per facta praesidentium cathedrae intrat, fiet *filius gehennae* magis quam illi, et requiescentibus universis qui ante sabbatum manna collegerunt, ille cum onere suo invenietur in die sabbati, in quo non est manna colligere neque onus exponere. Quia nolunt audire vocem filii Dei clamantis in Ecclesia et dicentis: *Venite ad me omnes qui onerati estis, et ego vos requiescere faciam.*

Isti sunt fures qui non per ianuam veram sed per portas suas intrant in suam Hierusalem, et succendet Deus *ignem in portis Hierusalem,* et comburet *itinera* eius *et non extinguetur.* Ignis enim qui specialis Hierusalem portas exussit extinctus est; apostolus autem sabbatum et alia legis mandata figuram esse futuri sic ait: *Nemo ergo vos iudicet in cibo et potu aut in parte diei festi aut neomeniae aut sabbatorum, quod est umbra futuri.*

Multis in locis unius temporis diversi eventus in speciem separatim descripti duo tempora fecerunt, quasi ex ordine se insequentia; in genere autem uno tempore est uterque eventus. Sic XIIII anni sub Joseph ubertatis et sterilitatis VII anni sunt tantum, id est omne tempus a passione Domini, in cuius figura factus est Ioseph dominus Aegypti cum esset XXX annorum; qui sunt itaque nobis VII anni ubertatis et saturitatis, id est ceteris VII sterilitatis et famis. Isto enim tempore minatur Dominus divitibus famem, pauperibus vero saturitatem promittit. Haec bona et mala duplicis temporis uno tempore futura testatur Scriptura Exodi, qua manifestum est omnium plagarum Aegypti immunem fuisse

Lord knows those who are his."[1] If anyone entered through the precepts of those who preside in Moses' seat,[2] he enters through Christ—for the precepts are his. He puts down the burden of his sins and, without it, enters the sabbath rest. If anyone enters not through the precepts but through the deeds of those who preside in that seat, he will be even more "a child of hell"[3] than they; and, while all those who gathered manna before the sabbath are at rest, he will be discovered still carrying his burden on the sabbath day, when there is no gathering of manna or putting down of burdens.[4] For they are not willing to listen to the voice of the son of God crying out in the church to say: "come to me all you who are burdened, and I will give you rest."[5]

These are the thieves who do not enter through the true door,[6] but enter their own Jerusalem through their own gates; and God will light "a fire in the gates of Jerusalem," and it will consume its "streets and will not be quenched."[7] For, at the level of the particular, the fire that burned the gates of Jerusalem was quenched; but the apostle indicates that the sabbath and the other commandments of the law are a figure of what is to come: "therefore let no one pass judgment on you on matters of food and drink or with respect to a festival or a new moon or the sabbath, which is a shadow of what is to come."[8]

In many passages, the diverse events of a single time span, depicted separately at the level of the particular, create two periods of time, the one following the other, so to speak, in sequence. At the level of the general, however, both events belong to one time. Thus the 14 years of plenty and of blight under Joseph[9] actually make only 7 years, i.e., the whole span of time following the passion of the Lord, as a figure of whom Joseph became lord of Egypt when he was thirty years old.[10] For us, therefore, these are 7 years of plenty and repleteness; i.e., it is for others that they are 7 years of blight and famine. For the Lord threatens the rich with famine in that time; but to the poor he promises that they will be full.[11] The book of Exodus testifies that these goods and evils, spread across a double time span, will belong to one period of time, since it is manifest that Israel was immune to all the plagues on Egypt and

---

[1]2 Tim. 2:19

[2]See Mt. 23:2.

[3]Mt. 23:15

[4]See Ex. 16:22-30.

[5]Mt. 11:28

[6]The allusion is to Jn. 10:1, 7.

[7]Jer. 17:27

[8]Col. 2:16-17

[9]Gen. 41:26ff.

[10]Gen. 41:46

[11]The allusion is to Lk. 6:20-21, 24-25.

Israhel, et per tres dies tenebrarum lumen habuisse. Quod nunc spiritaliter geritur, sicut Deus eidem Faraoni postea comminatus est dicens: *Dabo tenebras super terram tuam.*

Aliquotiens unum tempus in multas diuidet partes, quarum singulae totum tempus sint. Sic annus quo fuit Noe in arca dividitur inter omnes numeros. Quotiens tamen temporum mentio est, quaternarius numerus specialiter tempus est a Domini passione usque in finem. Quaternarius est autem quotiens aut plenus est, aut post tertium pars quarti ut CCCL aut tres et dimidium. Ceteri vero numeri pro locis intellegendi sunt; signa sunt enim, non manifestae definitiones. XL ergo dies diluvii tempus est. Nam isti sunt CCCC anni in Aegypto, et XL anni in heremo, et XL dies ieiunii Domini et Moysi et Heliae, quibus in heremo ieiunat Ecclesia, id est abstinet a mortuorum voluptatibus; id est XL dies quibus mandacat et bibit Ecclesia cum Domino post resurrectionem, id est XL anni quibus erat Ecclesia *manducans et bibens* sub Salomone, pace undique versum profunda, premente tamen eodem bipertito Salomone, sicut eadem Ecclesia dicit: *Pater tuus oppressit nos.* XL dies fuit aqua statu suo et totidem defecit dies, et defectio aquae decimo mense, id est perfecto tempore, completur. Sed in genere non ita est, ut quodam tempore invalescat et deinde deficiat: quoniam quo tempore invalescit carnaliter eodem deficit spiritaliter, ut ipsa elatio sit defectio usque dum perficiatur tempus, sicut mundus regnans ponitur sub pedibus Ecclesiae, id est filii hominis. Qui sunt itaque XL dies, id est CL, in Ezechiel; namque XL

had light throughout the three days of darkness.[1] This now happens spiritually, just as God later threatened the same pharaoh when he said, "I will put darkness over your land."[2]

Often he will divide one period of time into many parts, of which each one represents the whole time. Thus the year Noah spent in the ark is divided among all sorts of numbers.[3] Nevertheless, so often as there is mention of periods of time, the number four in particular represents the time from the Lord's passion to the end. Moreover, it is the number four whenever it appears either in full or as part of a fourth after three, for example, 350 or three and a half. The other numbers, to be sure, must be understood according to the context; for they are signs, not open equivalents. The time of the flood, therefore, is 40 days.[4] For these are the 400 years in Egypt, and the 40 years in the wilderness, and the 40 days of the Lord's fast and Moses' and Elijah's,[5] during which the church fasts in the wilderness, i.e., abstains from desires for things that are dead; that is, the 40 days during which the church eats and drinks with the Lord after his resurrection;[6] that is, the 40 years during which the church was "eating and drinking"[7] under Solomon in deep peace on all sides, yet with the same bipartite Solomon oppressing it, as the same church says: "your father oppressed us."[8] The flood lasted 40 days, and for as many days it receded.[9] And the receding of the water was completed in the tenth month,[10] i.e., the time of perfection. At the level of the general, however, it does not happen that the water increases for a certain time and then recedes: rather, at the same time that it is increasing with respect to the carnal it is receding with respect to the spiritual. As a result, the increase is itself the receding until the time is complete, just as the world and its rule are being put under the feet of the church, i.e., of the son of man. These are, therefore, the 40 days, i.e., the 150 days,[11] in Ezekiel; for he discharged the sins of Judah for 40 days and the sins

---

[1] Tyconius' point is that the periods of plenty and famine, apparently successive, are actually concurrent. They apply, however, to different groups: the famine to Egypt, the plenty to Israel. This now happens spiritually in that, spiritually, the faithful now have plenty while the unfaithful have famine. Materially, of course, the situation may be quite the opposite.

[2] Ezek. 32:8

[3] See Gen. 7-8.

[4] See Gen. 7:4, 17.

[5] See Mt. 4:2, Ex. 34:28 and 1 Kings 19:8.

[6] See Acts 1:3, 4.

[7] 1 Kings 2:46a (cf. Septuagint)

[8] 1 Kings 12:24p (cf. Septuagint)

[9] See Gen. 7:17, 8:6.

[10] See Gen. 8:5.

[11] See Gen. 7:17, 24.

diebus exsolvit peccata Iuda, et Israhel CL, quod est unum atque idem. Et *septimo mense sedit arca,* idem tempus; et *deficiebat aqua usque in decimum mensem,* idem tempus. Exivit de arca duodecimo mense; hic est *annus* libertatis *Domini acceptabilis,* quo completo manifestabitur Ecclesia mundi pertransisse diluvium.

Unaquaeque pars huius anni idem annus est. Quale si diceret, Exivit de arca quadragesimo die, aut, Mense septimo aut decimo; sunt enim istae partes recapitulationis ab initio usque in finem. Sicut ab Adam usque Enoc, id est Ecclesiae translationem, VII generationes, quod est omne tempus; rursum ab Adam usque ad Noe, id est mundi reparationem, X generationes, quod est omne tempus; et a Noe usque ad Abraham X generationes. Nam et C anni quibus arca fabricata est omne tempus est quo Ecclesia fabricatur, et eo tempore in diluvio pereuntibus universis gubernatur.

Quod prudentibus plenius investigandum data via relinquimus; quoniam, ne copia Scripturae foret in interpretando et ea quae hunc intellectum forte impediunt removendo, singula persequenda non putavimus alio properantes.

VI. De recapitulatione

Inter regulas quibus Spiritus legem signavit quo luminis via custodiretur, non nihil custodit recapitulationis sigillum ea subtilitate, ut continuatio magis narrationis quam recapitulatio videatur.

Aliquotiens enim sic recapitulat: Tunc, Illa hora, Illo die, Eo tempore; sicuti Dominus loquitur in Evangelio dicens: *Die quo exiit Loth a Sodomis pluit ignem de caelo et perdidit omnes; secundum haec erit dies filii hominis, quo revelabitur. Illa hora qui erit in tecto et vasa eius in domo non descendat tollere illa, et qui in agro similiter non revertatur retro, meminerit uxoris Loth.* Numquid illa hora qua Dominus revelatus fuerit adventu suo

of Israel for 150, which is one and the same.[1]   And "in the seventh
month the ark came to rest,"[2] the same time; and "the water receded
until the tenth month,"[3] the same time. He went out from the ark in the
twelfth month; this is "the acceptable year" of the freedom "of the Lord,"[4]
and when it is complete the church will be shown to have passed
through the flood of the world.

Any part of this year represents this same year: if it were to say, for
instance, "he went out from the ark on the fortieth day," or in the
seventh month or in the tenth. For these are parts of a recapitulation that
goes from the beginning to the end. So from Adam to Enoch—i.e., the
translation of the church—there were 7 generations, which represents
all time; and again from Adam to Noah—i.e., the restoration of the
world—there were 10 generations, which represents all time; and from
Noah to Abraham, 10 generations. For, too, the 100 years during which
the ark was built represent all time, during which the church is being
built; and during that time, while everything is perishing in the flood,
its helm is manned.

Now that we have shown the way, we leave aside the matters that
require further investigation on the part of the wise. Lest the wealth of
scripture depend on explaining and removing the things that might
impede this understanding, we have not supposed that we need to pursue
individual details when we are quickly moving on to another point.

VI. Recapitulation

Among the rules with which the Spirit has sealed the law so as to
guard the pathway of light, the seal of recapitulation guards some things
with such subtlety that it seems more a continuation than a recapitulation of the narrative.

For the recapitulation often takes this form: "then," "in that hour,"
"on that day," "at that time." For example, in the gospel the Lord says,
"on the day Lot left Sodom, it rained fire from heaven and destroyed
them all. The day of the son of man, when he is revealed, will be the
same. At that hour, anyone who is on the housetop, with his possessions
in the house, must not come down to collect them, and so too anyone who
is in the field must not turn back. He should remember Lot's wife."[5]   Is
it only at the hour when the Lord is revealed in his coming[6] that a

---

[1]See Ezek. 4:4-6. The Septuagint has 150 days for Israel.

[2]Gen. 8:4

[3]Gen. 8:5

[4]Lk. 4:19, apparently conflated with 2 Cor. 6:2.

[5]Lk. 17:29-32

[6]The Lord's final coming, it would seem, rather than his continuous coming
in his body, the church.

non debet quis converti ad ea quae sua sunt et uxoris Loth meminisse, et
non antequam reveletur? Dominus autem illa hora qua revelatus fuerit
iussit ista observari, non solum ut abscondendo quaerentibus gratiorem
faceret ueritatem, sed etiam ut totum illud tempus diem vel horam esse
monstraret.   Eadem itaque hora, id est tempore, ista observanda
mandavit, sed antequam reveletur: eadem quidem hora, sed in qua parte
horae ratione cognoscitur.

Aliquotiens autem non sunt recapitulationes huius modi sed futurae
similitudines, sicut Dominus dicit: *Cum videritis quod dictum est per
Danihelem prophetam, tunc qui in Iudaea sunt fugiant in montes*, et inducit
finem.   Quod autem Danihel dixit in Africa geritur, neque in eodem
tempore finis.   Sed quoniam, licet non in eo tempore finis, in eo tamen
titulo futurum est, propterea *Tunc* dixit, id est cum similiter factum fuerit
per orbem, quod est *discessio* et *revelatio hominis peccati*. Hoc genere
locutionis dicit Spiritus in Psalmis: *Cum averteret Dominus captivitatem
Sion facti sumus velut consolati.   Tunc repletum est gaudio os nostrum et
lingua nostra exultatione.   Tunc dicent in gentibus: Magnificavit Dominus
facere cum illis, magnificavit Dominus facere nobiscum, facti sumus
laetantes.* Dicendum erat: Cum averterit Dominus captivitatem Sion, tunc
dixerunt in gentibus; nunc autem: *Cum averteret* inquit *tunc dicent in
gentibus.* Nos enim gentes quorum captivitatem avertit. Sicut et illorum
in figuram tempus habemus dicentes: *Magnificavit Dominus facere cum
eis, magnificavit Dominus facere nobiscum.* De similitudine itaque tempus
suum et nostrum unum fecit et iunxit dicens: *Tunc dicent in gentibus*, id
est cum similiter gentibus fecerit.

Nec illud praetereundum puto, quod Spiritus sine mysteriis vel
allegoria aliud sonare aliud intellegi voluit, sicut per Iohannem: *Multi
pseudoprophetae prodierunt in hoc mundo.   In isto cognoscite Spiritum Dei:
omnis spiritus qui soluit Iesum et negat in carne venisse de Deo non est, sed
hic de antichristo est, quod audistis quoniam venit, et nunc in isto mundo
praesens est.*   Numquid omnis qui non negat Iesum in carne venisse

person ought not to turn back for his belongings and ought to have remembered Lot's wife—and not also before he is revealed? But the Lord commanded that these things be observed at the hour of his revelation not only to enhance the value of the truth, for those who seek it, by making it hard to find, but also to show that that whole time is the "day" or the "hour." Thus he commanded that these things are to be observed at that same hour, i.e., time, but before he is revealed: at that same hour, to be sure, but reason discerns in which part of the hour.

Often, too, recapitulations are not of this sort, but appear as a likeness of what is to come, as when the Lord says, "when you see what was mentioned in the prophet Daniel, then let those in Judea take flight to the mountains,"[1] and goes on to speak of the end. But what Daniel mentioned is happening now in Africa,[2] and not at the time of the end. But because this was going to happen, although not at the time of the end, yet under the same heading, he said, "then," i.e., when similar things happen through the world, which is the "departure" and the "revelation of the man of sin."[3] Using this kind of expression, the Spirit says in the Psalms: "When the Lord ended Sion's captivity, we were like people consoled. Then was our mouth filled with joy and our tongue with rejoicing. Then will they say among the nations: the Lord has done marvels for them, the Lord has done marvels for us, we were overjoyed."[4] It ought to have said, "when the Lord ended Sion's captivity, then they said among the nations"; but in fact it has, "when he ended . . . then will they say among the nations." For we are the nations whose captivity he ended. And so, too, we have the same temporal position as those in the figure, saying: "the Lord has done marvels for them, the Lord has done marvels for us." Due to the likeness, therefore, he treated their time and ours as one and joined them together in saying, "then will they say among the nations," i.e., when he does similar things for the nations.

Nor do I think that we should overlook the point that, even without mysteries and allegory, the Spirit wanted one thing to sound forth, another to be understood; for example, in John: "many false prophets have appeared in this world. By this you will know the Spirit of God: any spirit that rejects Jesus and denies that he has come in the flesh is not from God, but is rather from antichrist. You have heard that he was coming; and now he is present in this world."[5] Does everyone who does not deny that Jesus has come in the flesh have the Spirit of God? Rather,

---

[1] Mt. 24:15, 16

[2] Again it is impossible to know precisely what events or circumstances Tyconius may have had in mind, although the general reference is surely to the conflict between Donatist and catholic Christians.

[3] 2 Thess. 2:3

[4] Ps. 126:1-3

[5] 1 Jn. 4:1-3

Spiritum Dei habet? Sed hanc negationem in opere non in voce esse, et unumquemque non ex professione sed ex fructibus intellegi debere, in omni ipsa epistula, qua non nisi de fratribus bonis et malis scripsit, subtiliter admonet eodem genere locutionis, sicut dicit: *In isto cognoscimus quoniam cognovimus eum, si praecepta eius custodiamus. Qui autem dicit quoniam cognovit eum, et mandata eius non servat, mendax est.* Numquid ex professione dixit intellegi fratrem qui Deum nescit, et non ex operibus? Et iterum: *Qui dicit se in luce esse, et fratrem suum odit, in tenebris est usque adhuc. Et iterum: Qui dixerit quoniam diligit Deum, et fratrem suum odit, mendax est.* Si enim ut dicit diligit Deum, doceat operibus, adhaereat Deo, diligat Deum in fratre. Si credit Christum incarnatum, quiescat odisse membra Christi. Si credit Verbum carnem factum, quid persequitur Verbum in carne? Si credit quod dixit Dominus: *Quamdiu fecistis uni ex istis fratribus meis minimis in me credentibus, mihi fecistis,* non operetur malum Christo in carne, id est in servis eius, quoniam Dominus et Ecclesia *una caro* est. In qua carne si credit esse hominem, cur non diligit, aut—quod crudelius est—cur odit, sicut scriptum est: *Qui non diligit fratrem suum permanet in morte,* et: *Qui fratrem suum odit homicida est?* Aliud maius et evidentius signum agnoscendi antichristi non esse dixit, quam qui negat Christum in carne, id est odit fratrem.

Tale est autem quod dicit: *Quoniam qui non negaverit Christum in carne de Deo est,* quale: *Nemo potest dicere Dominum Iesum, nisi in Spiritu Sancto,* cum multi dicant Dominum Iesum, ipso contestante: *Non omnis qui mihi dicit Domine Domine introibit in regnum caelorum.* Sed hoc loco apostolus neminem posse *dicere Dominum Iesum nisi in Spiritu Sancto* secundum conscientiam dixit, *secundum interiorem hominem* non secundam solam

through this whole epistle—where he wrote about nothing else but the good and the evil brothers—he subtly warns us, using this same kind of expression, that this denial is a matter of works, not words, and that each individual must be understood by the fruit he bears, not the words he says. For example, he says: "by this we can be sure that we know him: if we keep his commandments. Anyone who says that he knows him and does not keep his commandments is a liar."[1] Did he say that the brother who does not know God is recognized by what he says and not by his works? And again: "anyone who claims that he is in the light and hates his brother is still in the dark."[2] And again: "anyone who says that he loves God and hates his brother is a liar."[3] For if he does love God as he says, let him show it by his works. Let him cling to God.[4] Let him love God in his brother. If he believes in Christ incarnate, let him stop hating the members of Christ. If he believes the Word became flesh, why does he persecute the Word in the flesh? If he believes what the Lord said, "insofar as you did this to one of the least of these, my brothers, who believe in me, you did it to me,"[5] let him do no evil to Christ in the flesh, i.e., in his servants. For the Lord and the church are "one flesh."[6] If he believes that a person is in that flesh, why does he not love him or—crueler still—why does he hate him, when it is written, "anyone who does not love" his brother "remains in death," and "anyone who hates his brother is a murderer"?[7] He has declared that there is no greater or plainer sign for recognizing antichrist than a person who denies Christ in the flesh, i.e., who hates his brother.

Moreover this saying—"anyone who does not deny Christ in the flesh is from God"[0]—has the same import as "no one can say Jesus is Lord except in the Holy Spirit,"[9] even though there are many who call Jesus Lord, as he himself attests: "not everyone who says to me, Lord, Lord, will enter the kingdom of heaven."[10] In this passage, however, the apostle declared that "no one can say Jesus is Lord except in the Holy Spirit" when the person is speaking in conscience, "according to the inmost self,"[11] and not according to mere words alone. He said this in

---

[1] 1 Jn. 2:3-4
[2] 1 Jn. 2:9
[3] 1 Jn. 4:20
[4] The allusion is to Ps. 73:28.
[5] Mt. 25:40, apparently conflated with Mt. 18:6.
[6] Eph. 5:31
[7] 1 Jn. 3:14-15
[8] 1 Jn. 4:2
[9] 1 Cor. 12:3
[10] Mt. 7:21
[11] Rom. 7:22

professionem, ut ostenderet illis qui credunt Dominum Iesum nihil minus habere ab his qui charismatum generibus extolluntur, sed unum atque eundem Spiritum possidere omnem qui Iesum Dominum corde crediderit, id est operibus credidisse monstraverit. *Nemo* inquit *potest dicere Dominum Iesum nisi in Spiritu Sancto. Divisiones autem charismatum sunt, Idem autem Spiritus; divisiones mysteriorum, et idem Dominus.*

Solvere autem *Iesum* est non facere quod Iesum fecisse confitetur, sicut idem Dominus dicit: *Qui solverit unum ex mandatis istis minimis, et sic docuerit homines, minimus vocabitur in regno caelorum.* Et quid sit *Solverit* consequentibus aperit dicens: *Qui* autem *fecerit et sic docuerit.*

Hanc ergo negationem operum esse non vocis et Paulus apostolus confirmat dicens: *Deum scire confitentur, factis autem negant.* Et iterum: *Habentes deformationem pietatis, virtutem autem eius negantes.* Hoc sensu dicit *quosdam* fratres *non sancte Christum praedicare*—sed corde, nam voce sancta praedicabant. Consentit denique praedicationi eorum et mandat audiri dicens: *Quid interest? Omni modo sive per occasionem sive per veritatem Christus adnuntietur.* Dominum autem Christum antichristus non voto sed occasione praedicabat. Alio tendens per Christi nomen ingreditur, quo sibi viam sternat, quo sub Christi nomine ventri pareat, et his—quae turpe est dicere—sanctitatis et simplicitatis nomen imponat, signis et prodigiis *cubiculorum* opera Christum esse asseverans. Quos salubri cautione vitare admonet apostolus dicens: *Filioli, abstinete vos a simulacris.*

VII. De diabolo et corpore eius.

Diaboli et corporis eius ratio breviter videri potest, si id quod de Domino et eius corpore dictum est in hoc quoque observetur. Transitus namque a capite ad corpus eadem ratione dinoscitur, sicut per Esaiam de

order to show those who believe Jesus is Lord that they have no lower standing than those who are distinguished by all kinds of spiritual gifts. Rather, everyone who believes in his heart that Jesus is Lord, i.e., who shows his belief in works, has one and the same Spirit. "No one," he says, "can say Jesus is Lord except in the Holy Spirit. There are various gifts, but the same Spirit; various mysteries, and the same Lord."[1]

Now to "reject Jesus"[2] is not to do what one confesses that Jesus did; as the same Lord declares, "anyone who rejects one of the least of these commandments, and teaches others the same, will be called least in the kingdom of heaven."[3] And he indicates what "rejects" means when he goes on to say, "anyone who" does this "and teaches others the same."

Thus, too, the apostle Paul confirms that this denial is a matter of works, not of words, when he says, "they claim to know God, but they deny him with their deeds."[4] And again: "they have the appearance of religion, but deny its power."[5] It is in this sense that he says that "some" of the brothers "do not proclaim Christ purely"—but he means in heart, for the words of their preaching were holy. Consequently he consents to their preaching and commands that it be heard, when he says: "what difference does it make? By all means, whether in pretense or in truth, let Christ be proclaimed."[6] Thus antichrist was proclaiming Christ as Lord not in honesty but in pretense. With something quite different in mind, he enters in Christ's name in order to smooth the way for himself, in order to indulge his belly[7] under the name of Christ; and to these actions—it is shameful to say—he gives the name of purity and simplicity, asserting with signs and wonders that the works of the bedroom represent Christ.[8] With salutary caution, the apostle warns us to avoid such people: "little children, keep away from mere semblances."[9]

VII. The Devil and His Body

The relation of the devil and his body can be conceived in short order, if we keep in mind, here also, what we have said about the Lord and his body. The transition from head to body is recognized by the same kind of reasoning. For example, in Isaiah, this is said of the king of

---

[1] 1 Cor. 12:3-5

[2] 1 Jn. 4:3

[3] Mt. 5:19

[4] Titus 1:16

[5] 2 Tim. 3:5

[6] Phil. 1:17-18

[7] The allusion is to Phil. 3:19.

[8] Perhaps an allusion to Mt. 24:24, 26.

[9] 1 Jn. 5:21

rege Babylonis: *Quomodo cecidit de caelo lucifer mane oriens! Contritus est in terra qui mittit ad omnes gentes! Tu autem dixisti in animo tuo: In caelum ascendam, super stellas Dei ponam sedem meam, sedebo in monte alto super montes altos in Aquilonem, ascendam super nubes, ero similis Altissimo. Nunc autem ad inferos descendes in fundamenta terrae, et qui viderint te mirabuntur super te et dicent: Hic est homo qui concitat terram, movet reges; qui ponit orbem terrae totum desertum, civitates autem destruxit abductosque non solvit. Omnes reges gentium dormierunt in honore, homo in domu sua; tu autem proiectus es in montes velut mortuus abominatus cum omnibus qui ceciderunt inserti gladio et descendunt ad inferos. Quomodo vestimentum sanguine consparsum non erit mundum, ita nec tu eris mundus, quia terram meam perdidisti et plebem meam occidisti. Non eris in aeternum tempus semen nequam; para filios tuos interfici peccatis patris tui, ut non resurgant.* In rege Babylonis et omnes reges et omnis populus significatur, unum est enim corpus.

Quomodo inquit *cecidit de caelo lucifer mane oriens! Confractus est in terra qui mittit ad omnes gentes! Tu autem dixisti in animo tuo: In caelum ascendam, super stellas Dei ponam sedem meam.* Diabolus hoc sibi non promittit; non enim sperat renitendo posse in caelum ascendere, qui ne deiceretur resistere non valuit. Multo magis ista homo sperare non potest; tamen hominem esse sic dicit: *Hic est homo qui incitat terram.* Sed praeter hanc rationem qua neque diabolus neque homo sperare potest se posse in caelum ascendere et super stellas Dei sedens similem se Deo fieri, etiam ipsa Scriptura aliud inquirendum admonet. Nam si in caelo et supra stellas Dei dicit sedem suam positurum, quomodo in monte alto sedebit aut super montes in Aquilone uel in nubibus, ut similis sit Altissimo? Non enim Altissimus in huius modi habet sedem.

Caelum Ecclesiam dicit, sicut procedente Scriptura videbimus. De hoc caelo cadit lucifer matutinus; lucifer enim bipertitum est, cuius pars sancta est, sicut Dominus dicit in Apocalypsi de se et suo corpore: *Ego sum radix et genus David et stella splendida matutina, sponsus et sponsa.* Item

Babylon: "how the daystar, rising in the morning, has fallen from heaven! The one who sends out to all the nations has been crushed on the earth! You said in your heart: I will ascend to heaven, I will set my throne above the stars of God, I will sit on the high mountain above the high mountains to the north, I will rise above the clouds, I will be like the Most High. But now you will go down to the underworld in the depths of the earth. All who see you will stare at you in amazement and will say: this is the man who makes the earth tremble, who shakes kings, who makes the whole world a desert; he destroyed cities and did not loose his captives' bonds. All the kings of the nations lay in honor, each man in his own house. But you have been cast out on the mountains, despised like a dead man, along with all who fell, run through by the sword, and who are going down to the underworld. As a garment spattered with blood will not come clean, neither will you be clean, for you have brought my land to ruin and have killed my people. Your evil lineage will not last for ever. Prepare your sons to be killed for the sins of your father so that they never rise again."[1] In the king of Babylon are signified both all kings and all the people, for it is one body.

"How the daystar, rising in the morning, has fallen from heaven! The one who sends out to all the nations has been broken to pieces on earth! You said in your heart: I will ascend to heaven, I will set my throne above the stars of God."[2] The devil promises himself no such thing. He was not strong enough to resist being cast down; and he retains no hope that he can ascend to heaven by striving once again. Even less can a man have such hopes. Yet it says that this is a man: "this is the man who makes the earth tremble."[3] But beyond this reasoning, according to which neither devil nor man can hope to be able to ascend to heaven and, enthroned above the stars of God, be like God, scripture itself also admonishes us to make inquiry on another point. For, if he says that he will set his throne in heaven and above the stars of God, how is he going to sit on the high mountain or above the high mountains to the north or on the clouds so as to be like the Most High. For the Most High has no such seat.

As we shall see as scripture proceeds, it is the church that he calls "heaven." And it is from this heaven that the morning daystar falls. For the daystar is bipartite; and one part is holy, as the Lord says in the Apocalypse, speaking of himself and his own body, "I am the root and the offspring of David, and the bright morning star, bridegroom and bride."[4] Likewise, in the same book: "those who win the victory, to them I will

---

[1] Is. 14:12-21
[2] Is. 14:12-13
[3] Is. 14:16
[4] Rev. 22:16-17

illic: *Qui vincit, dabo illi stellam matutinam,* id est ut sit stella matutina sicut Christus, quem accepimus. Pars ergo luciferi, id est adversum corpus quod est diabolus reges et populus, cadit de caelo et confringitur in terra. His regibus dicit Sapientia: *Audite ergo reges et intellegite, discite iudices finium terrae, praebete aures qui continetis multitudinem et placetis vobis in turbis nationum. Quoniam data est vobis potestas a Domino, et virtus ab Altissimo, qui interrogabit opera vestra, et cogitationes scrutabitur; quoniam cum essetis ministri regni illius non recte iudicastis, neque custodistis legem.*

Rex ergo Babylonis totum corpus est, sed pro locis intellegemus in quam partem corporis conveniat. *Cecidit de caelo lucifer* in omne corpus potest convenire; *In caelum ascendam, super stellas Dei ponam sedem meam* similiter in caput et maiores qui stellarum Dei, id est sanctorum, dominandum putant, cum ipsorum minores dominentur sicut scriptum est: *Maior serviet minori.* Huic Esau, id est fratribus malis, sic dicit Dominus per Abdiam prophetam: *Exaltans habitationem suam, dicens in corde suo: Quis me deducet ad terram? Si exaltatus fueris sicut aquila, et inter stellas ponas nidum tuum, inde detraham te, dicit Dominus.*

Sedebo in monte alto super montes altos in Aquilonem, ascendam super nubes, ero similis Altissimo. Mons altus populus est superbus; *montes alti* singuli quique superbi, qui adunati montem faciunt, id est corpus diaboli. Multos enim esse montes malos sic dicit Scriptura: *Transferuntur montes in cor maris.* Et iterum: *Fundamenta montium conturbata sunt et commota sunt, quoniam iratus est eis Deus.* Nam et si corpus Domini id est Ecclesia mons dicitur, et singuli qui Ecclesiam faciunt montes, sicut scriptum est: *Ego autem constitutus sum rex ab eo super Sion montem sanctum eius adnuntians imperia eius.* Et iterum: *Perdam Assyrios in terra mea et in*

give the morning star,"[1] i.e., so they may be the morning star like Christ whom we have received. It is therefore a part of the daystar—i.e., the enemy body which consists of devil, kings and people—that falls from heaven and is broken to pieces on earth. To these kings wisdom says: "listen then, kings, and understand; learn, you judges of the ends of the earth; pay attention, you who hold sway over multitudes and plume yourselves among the throngs of the nations. Your power was given to you by the Lord and your strength by the most High; he will inspect your works and put your designs under scrutiny. For you, although ministers of his kingdom, have not judged rightly, nor have you kept the law."[2]

Thus the king of Babylon represents the whole body. But it is according to the context that we understand to which part of the body he pertains. "The daystar has fallen from heaven" can pertain to the entire body. Similarly "I will ascend to heaven, I will set my throne above the stars of God" can pertain to the head and to the elders who suppose that it is for them to rule over the stars of God, i.e., the saints, when in fact the younger will rule over them, as it is written: "the elder will serve the younger."[3] To this Esau, i.e., to the evil brothers, the Lord speaks in this way through the prophet Obadiah: "raising his dwelling on high, saying in his heart: who will bring me down to earth? Though you rise up like the eagle and set your nest among the stars, I will bring you down, says the Lord."[4]

"I will sit on the high mountain above the high mountains to the north, I will rise above the clouds, I will be like the Most High."[5] The "high mountain" is a people puffed up with pride; the "high mountains" are all the individuals puffed up with pride. Joined together, they make the mountain, i.e., the devil's body. For that there are many evil mountains, scripture states in the following way: "the mountains are carried into the heart of the sea."[6] And again: "the foundations of the mountains trembled and shook, for God was angry at them."[7] For, even if the Lord's body, i.e., the church, is called a mountain, the individuals who make up the church are also called mountains, as it is written: "by him was I made king on Zion, his holy mountain, proclaiming his decrees."[8] And again: "I will destroy the Assyrians in my land and on

---

[1]Rev. 2:26, 28
[2]Wisd. 6:1-4
[3]Gen. 25:23 (cf. Rom. 9:12-13)
[4]Obad. 3-4
[5]Is. 14:13-14
[6]Ps. 46:2
[7]Ps. 18:7
[8]Ps. 2:6-7

montibus meis. Et iterum: *Suscipiant montes pacem populo tuo et colles.* Et iterum: *Montes exultabunt velut arietes, et colles velut agni ovium.* Deus in monte Sion habet sedem et in montibus Israhel et in nubibus sanctis suis, quod est Ecclesia, sicut scriptum est: *Timeat a facie Domini omnis terra, quoniam exsurrexit de nubibus sanctis.* Et iterum: *Nubibus mandabo ne pluant super eam imbrem* Iterum: *Nimbus et nubes in circuitu eius.* Et quod in monte Sion habitet sic dicit: *Cognoscetis quoniam ego sum Dominus Deus vester, habitans in Sion monte sancto meo.* Et diabolus in monte sedet, sed Seir qui est Esau, id est fratrum malorum, quem montem Deus increpat per Ezechielem, et dicit *in laetitia universae terrae desolaturum,* quod adversum Iacob inimicitias exerceat. Ipse est mons, ipsi montes Aquilonis. In his diabolus sedet, et nubium caeli veluti dominatur; hactenus se similem dicit Altissimo.

Duae sunt partes in Ecclesia, Austri et Aquilonis, id est meridiana et septentrionalis. In parte meridiana Dominus manet, sicut scriptum est: *Ubi pascis, ubi manes in meridiano.* Diabolus vero in Aquilone, sicut dicit Dominus populo suo: *Illum ab Aquilone persequar a vobis, et expellam illum in terram sine aqua*—id est in suos—*et exterminabo faciem eius in mare primum, et posteriora eius in mare novissimum,* quod est in populos primos et novissimos. Ad instar Ecclesiae fabricatus est iste mundus, in quo sol oriens non nisi per Austrum, id est meridianum, iter habet, et decursa Australi parte invisibilis vadit in locum suum rediens. Sic Dominus noster Iesus Christus sol aeternus partem suam percurrit, unde et meridianum vocat. Aquiloni vero, id est adversae parti, non oritur, sicut idem cum in iudicium venerint dicent: *Iustitiae lumen non luxit nobis, et sol non ortus est nobis;* *Timentibus* autem Dominum *oritur sol iustitiae, et*

my mountains."[1] And again: "let the mountains and the hills bring peace for your people."[2] And again: "the mountains will leap like rams, and the hills like lambs."[3] God has his throne on Mount Zion and on the mountains of Israel and on his holy clouds, which are the church, as it is written: "let all the earth stand in fear before the Lord, for he has risen from his holy clouds."[4] And again: "I will command the clouds to rain no rain on it."[5] Again: "storm cloud and dark cloud surround him."[6] And that he dwells on Mount Zion, he declares in this way: "you will know that I am the Lord your God, dwelling on Zion, my holy mountain."[7] The devil also has his seat on a mountain, but on Seir, which is Esau, i.e., the mountain of the evil brothers. God rebukes this mountain through Ezekiel and says that he "will leave it desolate, to the joy of all the earth,"[8] because of its enmity to Jacob. This is the mountain, these the mountains of the north. On these the devil sits and rules, as it were, the clouds of heaven; to this extent he claims to be like the Most High.

There are two parts in the church, one of the south and one of the north. The Lord abides in the southern part, as it is written: "where you graze your flock, where you abide in the south."[9] But the devil abides in the north, as the Lord says to his people: "the invader from the north I will drive away from you and will force him out into a land without water"—i.e., into his own people—"and drive his vanguard into the first sea and his rearguard into the last sea,"[10] which means into the first people and the last. This world was constructed in the likeness of the church. In it the rising sun follows no other course than through the south and, once it has traversed the southern part, it moves unseen in returning to its place. So also our Lord Jesus Christ, the eternal sun, passes through his own part, which is why he refers to it, too, as the south. But for the north, i.e., for the enemy part, he does not rise, as these same people will report when they come to judgment: "the light of justice has not shone for us, and the sun did not rise for us."[11] "For those who fear" the Lord, however, "the sun of justice rises, and there is healing in

---

[1] Is. 14:25

[2] Ps. 72:3

[3] Ps. 114:4

[4] Zech. 2:13

[5] Is. 5:6

[6] Ps. 97:2

[7] Joel 3:17

[8] Ezek. 35:14. Ezek. 35:15 locates Seir in Edom; and Gen. 36:8 identifies Edom with Esau.

[9] Song 1:7

[10] Joel 2:20

[11] Wisd. 5:6

sanitas in pinnis eius, sicut scriptum est. Malis vero meridie nox erit, sicut scriptum est: *Dum sustinent ipsi lumen factae sunt illis tenebrae, dum sustinent fulgorem obscura nocte ambulaverunt; palpabunt sicut caecus parietem, et quasi cui non sunt oculi palpabunt, et cadent meridie quasi media nocte.* Iterum: *Occidet sol meridie et tenebricabit super terram dies luminis.* Iterum: *Propterea nox erit vobis de visione, et tenebrae vobis erunt ex divinatione, et occidet sol super prophetas, et obscurabit super eos dies luminis.*

Huic populo ex Austro comminatur Deus, sicut per Ezechielem Sor increpat dicens: *Spiritus Austri contrivit te.* Si etiam confringere permittit, dicens: *Exurge Aquilo, et veni Auster perfla hortum meum, et defluent unguenta mea,* exurgenti nequam spiritui resistit Spiritus Sanctus qui Domini hortum perflat, et eliciuntur unguenta, id est odor suavitatis offertur. Et per Ezechielem iterum ex reliquiis populi mali sic dicit Deus adducere super populum suum partem eiusdem populi, quod est mysterium facinoris: *Ecce ego super te Gog, principem Ros Mesoc et Tobel. Et congregabo te et deducam te et ponam te a novissimo Aquilone, et adducam te super montes Israhel; et perdam arcum tuum de manu tua sinistra, et sagittas tuas de manu tua dextera, et deiciam te super montes Israhel.* Hoc autem geritur a passione Domini, quoadusque de medio eiusdem mysterii facinoris discedat Ecclesia quae detinet, ut in tempore suo detegatur impietas, sicut apostolus dicit: *Et nunc quid detineat scitis, ut in suo tempore detegatur. Mysterium enim iam operatur facinoris, tantum ut qui detinet modo, quoad usque de medio fiat; et tunc revelabitur ille impius.* Et in Hieremia legimus peccatores Israhel in Aquilone conveniri, Domino dicente: *Vade et lege sermones istos ad Aquilonem et dic, Convertere ad me*

its wings,"[1] as it is written. But for the evil it will be night at midday, as it is written: "as they looked for light, darkness came upon them; as they looked for brightness, they walked in deep night. They will feel for the wall like a blind man; and like a man with no eyes they will feel their way. They will stumble at midday as if it were the middle of the night."[2]   Again: "the sun will set at midday, and the daylight will go dark upon the earth."[3]   Again: "therefore you will have night without vision and darkness without divination; and the sun will set upon the prophets, and the daylight will darken over them."[4]

From the south God threatens this people, as when he rebukes Sor through Ezekiel and says, "the south wind has shattered you."[5] If he also permits it to wreak havoc—when he says, "arise, north wind; and come, south wind, blow through my garden, and my fragrances will waft down"[6]—the Holy Spirit, who blows through the Lord's garden, resists the rising evil spirit; and the fragrances are drawn out, i.e., a sweet odor is offered.[7]   And again through Ezekiel, God says that from the remnants of the evil people he will lead a part of that same people against his own people, which is the mystery of lawlessness:[8] "behold, I am against you, Gog, prince of Rosh, Meshech and Tubal.   And I will gather you and lead you forth and take you from the farthest reaches of the north; and I will lead you against the mountains of Israel.   And I will smash your bow from your left hand and your arrows from your right hand and dash you against the mountains of Israel."[9]   Now this goes on from the time of the Lord's passion until the church, which keeps it in check, withdraws from the midst of this mystery of lawlessness so that godlessness may be unveiled in its own time, as the apostle says: "and you now know what keeps it in check so that it may be unveiled in its own time.   For the mystery of lawlessness is already at work, only that what now keeps it in check does so until it passes from the midst; and then the godless one will be revealed."[10]   And in Jeremiah we read that the sinners of Israel are assembled in the north, when the Lord says, "go and read out these words to the north and say: turn back to me, house of Israel, says the

---

[1]Mal. 4:2

[2]Is. 59:9-10

[3]Amos 8:9

[4]Mic. 3:6

[5]Ezek. 27:26

[6]Song 4:16

[7]Perhaps an allusion to Eph. 5:2.

[8]The allusion is to 2 Thess. 2:7.

[9]Ezek. 39:1-4

[10]2 Thess. 2:6-8

domus Israhel, dicit Dominus. Meridianum vero pars est Domini, sicut et in Iob scriptum est: *A meridiana parte germinabit tibi vita;* Aquilo diaboli: utraque autem pars in toto mundo.

Ascendam inquit *super nubes, ero similis Altissimo. Nunc autem ad inferos descendes in fundamenta terrae. Qui viderint te mirabuntur super te et dicent: Hic est homo qui concitat terram, commovet reges, qui ponit orbem terrae totum desertum.* Numquid in diabolum convenit *Qui viderint te mirabuntur super te,* aut in regem novissimum cum ad inferos descenderit? Ipso enim ad inferos descendente non erit qui miretur mundo finito. Non enim dicent: Hic est homo qui incitavit terram, movit reges et posuit orbem terrae totum desertum, sed *Incitat* et *Commovet* et *Ponet.* Hominem enim totum corpus dicit tam in regibus quam in populis, cuius hominis superbi partem cum Deus percutit et ad inferos deicit dicimus: *Hic est homo qui incitat terram, commovet reges,* scilicet sanctos.

Qui ponit orbem terrae totum desertum. Irridentium vox est, non confirmantium, sicuti: *Qui dissolvit templum et in triduo illud suscitat!* Et: *Dixit enim: Fortitudine faciam, et sapientia intellectus auferam terminos nationum, et fortitudinem illarum vastabo, et comminuam civitates cum habitantibus; et totam orbem comprehendam manu velut nidum, et velut ova derelicta auferam, et non erit qui effugiat me aut contradicat mihi.* Numquid ista quae sibi promittit valet implere? *Ponit* quidem *orbem terrae totum desertum,* sed orbem suum; *Civitates autem destruxit,* utique sui orbis. Est enim bipertitus, mobilis et immobilis, sicut in Paralipomenon: *Commoveatur a facie Domini omnis terra. Etenim fundavit orbem terrae qui non commovebitur.*

Abductosque non solvit. Potest istud in speciem convenire, quod captivos in nullo relaxasset, sed immitis raptu aestimans principari tota

Lord."[1] The southern part, certainly, is the Lord's, as it is also written in Job: "from the southern part will your life sprout forth";[2] the north is the devil's. And both parts appear in all the world.[3]

"I will rise," it says, "above the clouds. I will be like the Most High. But now you will go down to the underworld in the depths of the earth. All who see you will stare at you in amazement and will say: this is the man who makes the earth tremble, who shakes kings, who makes the whole earth a desert."[4] Does the phrase, "all who see you will stare at you in amazement,"apply to the devil or to the last king as he descends to the underworld? When he descends to the underworld, there will be no one to stare in amazement. The world will have ended. For they are not going to say, "this is the man who made the earth tremble, shook kings and made the whole world a desert," but rather "makes" and "shakes" and "makes." He calls the whole body a man, kings as well as peoples. And when God strikes down a part of this man of pride and casts it into the underworld, we say, "this is the man who makes the earth tremble, who shakes kings," namely, the saints.

"Who makes the whole world a desert." Mockery speaks here, not consent. It is like: "he destroyed the temple and would rebuild it in three days!"[5] And: "for he said: by my strength I will do it, and in the wisdom of my understanding I will remove the boundaries of the nations and destroy their power and crush their cities and their inhabitants; and I will take the whole world in my hand like a bird's nest and carry it off like an abandoned bird's egg. And no one will escape me or go against my will."[6] Does he have the strength to carry out such ambitions? "He makes the whole world a desert," to be sure, but his own world; "he destroyed cities,"[7] the cities of his own world at any rate. For the world is bipartite, moving and unmoving, as in Chronicles: "let all the earth tremble before the Lord. For he has founded a world which will not be moved."[8]

"He did not loose his captives' bonds."[9] This can refer to the particular, in that he did nothing to ease his prisoners' lot but, a cruel man prizing rule by force, used all his power against them. This God

---

[1]Jer. 3:12

[2]Job 11:17

[3]Again Tyconius denies the Donatist claim that the true church ("the southern part") appears only in the Donatist communion in North Africa.

[4]Is. 14:14-17

[5]Mt. 27:40

[6]Is. 10:13-14

[7]Is. 14:17

[8]1 Chron. 16:30

[9]Is. 14:17

in eos uteretur potestate; quod obiurgat Deus dicens: *Ego quidem iratus sum modice, ipsi autem adiecerunt in mala.* Verumtamen in figuram generalitatis facta et dicta sunt, et spiritaliter implentur dum hi qui dominantur humilitatis subditos—aut temptationis causa uel merito sibi subditos—sine respectu pietatis atque communis conditionis affligunt, quibus non sufficit potestas, sed ea immoderatius uti contendunt, quod culpat dicens: *Persequentes retributionem,* et iterum: *Extendit manum suam ei in retribuendo.* Parum est enim quod inimicus est; adhuc gestit et in subditum vindicare, sicut scriptum est: *Omnes subditos uobis conpungitis;* dissimulans odisse Dominum *inimicum et uindicatorem,* quod per vindictam, quam soli sibi Deus exceptavit, aliquid deitatis usurpet. *Scriptum est enim: Mihi uindictam et ego retribuam, dicit Dominus.*

Omnes reges terrae dormierunt in honore, homo in domo sua. Reges sanctos dixit, nam non omnes reges vel privati in domo sua dormierunt, sicut sancti in domo quam delegerunt. *Tu autem proiectus es in montes uelut mortuus abominatus, cum omnibus qui ceciderunt inserti gladio et descendunt ad inferos.* Diabolo dicit *Proiectus es in montes,* in quibus sedet. Denique non dixit Mortuus, sed *Velut mortuus abominatus;* adhuc enim vivit, licet ipse in suis gladio perimatur et ad inferos descendat. Sicut enim Dominus quicquid sui patiuntur se pati dixit, ita et diabolus ipse in suis inculcatur, ipse abominatus confringitur, sicut scriptum est: *In diminutione populi comminutio principis.* Diabolus ab homine suo non separatur; nec homo in quo diabolus non est potest dicere: *Ero similis Altissimo,* nec de diabolo dici: *Hic homo qui incitat terram,* nisi in homine fuerit. Sicut Dominus homo non dici potest nisi in homine, nec homo

condemns, when he says, "I was only a little angry, but they have plunged into evil."[1] Nevertheless these things were done and said as figures of the general; and they are fulfilled spiritually so long as those who rule the lowly afflict their subjects—whether subject to them as a trial or by reason of what they deserve—without respect for God or the common condition. To such people, power is not enough; they want to use it without restraint. God censures this when he says, "they seek retribution,"[2] and again: "he stretched out his hand to him in retribution."[3] For it is not enough that he is an enemy; he still longs to take vengeance upon him also as a subject, as it is written: "you torment all your subjects."[4] He pretends it is not true that God hates "the enemy and the avenger"[5] because, through vengeance, which God reserved to himself alone, he usurps something of deity. "For it is written: vengeance is mine and I will pay back, says the Lord."[6]

"All the kings of the earth lay in honor, each man in his own house."[7] It is the saints that he called "kings," for not all kings or private individuals lay in their own house like the saints in the house they have chosen. "But you have been cast out on the mountains, despised like a dead man, along with all who fell, run through by the sword, and who are going down to the underworld."[8] To the devil he says, "you were cast out on the mountains," the mountains on which he has his seat. Then, too, he did not call him "dead," but "despised like a dead man"; for he still lives even though, in those who belong to him, he is himself killed by the sword and on his way down to the underworld. For just as the Lord said that he himself suffers anything that his people suffer,[9] so also the devil is himself trampled under foot in his people, is himself despised and ground to pieces, as it is written: "when the people decline, the prince is diminished."[10] The devil is not separate from the person who belongs to him. Unless the devil is in him, it is not possible for a man to say, "I will be like the Most High"; and unless he is in a man, it is not possible to say of the devil, "this is the man who makes the earth tremble."[11] So also the Lord cannot be called a man without

---

[1]Zech. 1:15
[2]Is. 1:23
[3]Ps. 55:20
[4]Is. 58:3
[5]Ps. 8:2
[6]Rom. 12:19
[7]Is. 14:18
[8]Is. 14:19
[9]See Mt. 25:34-46.
[10]Prov. 14:28
[11]Is. 14:14, 16

Deus nisi in Christo. Sed quid in quem conveniat pro locis obseruandum est.

Iterum in corpus ipsius diaboli convenit dicens: *Sicut vestimentum sanguine consparsum non est mundum, ita nec tu eris mundus, quia terram meam perdidisti et plebem meam occidisti. Non eris in aeternum tempus semen nequam; para fillos tuos interfici peccatis patris tui, ut non resurgant.* Hic ostendit non convenire in speciem. Rex enim Babylonis qui terram Domini vastavit et populum occidit, id est Nabuchodonosor, mundus obiit, in aeternum vivit; corpori dicit sui cuiusque temporis parare quos genuerit interfici peccatis eius, quo ipse qui convenitur genitus est. Novissimus enim rex non *filios* sed fratres habere potest, neque *velut mortuus* cum ad inferos descenderit, sed mortuus.

Per Ezechielem sic Deus increpat regem Tyri, id est omne corpus adversum: *Quoniam exaltatum est cor tuum, et dixisti: Deus sum ego, habitationem Dei habitavi in corde maris. Tu autem homo es et non Deus, et dedisti cor tuum tamquam cor Dei. Numquid sapientior es tu Danihele? Sapientes non arguerunt te sapientia sua? Numquid sapientia tua aut doctrina tua fecisti tibi virtutem, et aurum et argentum thesauris tuis? Numquid in multa doctrina tua et mercatu tuo multiplicasti virtutem tuam, et exaltatum est cor tuum in virtute tua? Propterea haec dicit Dominus, Quoniam dedisti cor tuum sicut cor Dei, propter hoc ecce ego induco super te alienos, pestes ex gentibus, et exinanient gladios suos super te et super decorem doctrinae tuae, et vulnerabunt decorem tuum in perditionem, et deponent te, et morieris morte vulneratorum in corde maris. Numquid dicturus es in conspectu interficientium te: Deus sum ego? Tu vero homo es et non Deus; in multitudine incircumcisorum peribis in manibus alienorum, quia ego locutus sum, dicit Dominus. Et factus est sermo Domini ad me dicens: Fili hominis, accipe lamentum super principem Tyri, et dic illi: haec dicit Dominus, Tu es signaculum similitudinis, et corona decoris in deliciis paradisi Dei fuisti, omnem lapidem optimum habens in te alligatum— sardium topazium smaragdum et carbunculum et saffirum et iaspin et argentum et aurum et ligyrium et achaten et amethystum chrysolithum et beryllum et onychinum—et auro replesti thesauros tuos et apothecas tuas in te. Ex qua die creatus es tu cum cherubim posui te in monte sancto Dei, fuisti in medio lapidum igneorum, abisti sine macula tu in diebus tuis ex qua die creatus es tu, donec invenirentur iniquitates tuae in te a multitudine negotiationis tuae. Implesti promptuaria tua iniquitate, et peccasti et*

being in a man, nor a man be called God without being in Christ. But what pertains to each must be determined according to the context.

It again pertains to the devil's body when it says: "As a garment spattered with blood will not come clean, neither will you be clean, for you have brought my land to ruin and have killed my people. Your evil lineage will not last for ever. Prepare your sons to be killed for the sins of your father so that they never rise again."[1] Here he shows that this does not pertain to the level of the particular. For the king of Babylon who devastated the Lord's land and killed the people, i.e., Nebuchadnezzar, was clean at his death and does have eternal life. It is rather his own body of every era that he tells to prepare the people it begets to be killed for the sins of him by whom the one mentioned was himself begotten. For the last king can have no "sons," only brothers, and is not "like a dead man" when he descends to the underworld, but actually dead.

Through Ezekiel God upbraids the king of Tyre, i.e., the whole enemy body, in this way: "your heart was puffed up, and you said: I am God, I dwelt in the dwelling of God in the heart of the sea. But you are a man and not God, and you made yourself out to be the equal of God. Are you wiser than Daniel? Have not the wise confuted you with their wisdom? Have you made yourself strong by your own wisdom or learning, or put gold and silver in your treasure houses? Have you multiplied your power in your great learning and your commerce and has your heart swelled at your power? Therefore thus says the Lord: because you made yourself out to be the equal of God, behold, I am bringing foreigners against you, a bane from the nations; and they will draw their swords against you and against the splendor of your learning and will wound your splendor to its ruin. They will throw you down; and you will die the death of the wounded in the heart of the sea. Face to face with your murderers, are you still going to say: I am God? In truth, you are a man and not God; you will perish at the hands of strangers in the throng of the uncircumcised, because I have spoken, says the Lord. And the word of the Lord came to me and said: son of man, raise a lament over the prince of Tyre and say to him: thus says the Lord, you are a sign of likeness, and you were the crowning splendor among the delights of God's paradise, set with every precious stone—carnelian, topaz, emerald, and carbuncle, and sapphire, and jasper, and silver, and gold, and jacinth, and agate, and amethyst, chrysolite, and beryl, and onyx—and you filled your treasure houses with gold and your storerooms within you. From the day of your creation I set you with the cherubim on God's holy mountain. You were among stones of fire; you lived your days without blame from the day of your creation until your iniquities were discovered from the vastness of your commerce. You filled your warehouses by evil dealings; and you

---

[1] Is. 14:20-21

vulneratus es a monte Dei, abduxit te cherubim de medio lapidum igneorum. Exaltatum est cor tuum in decore tuo, corrupta est doctrina tua cum decore tuo. Propter multitudinem peccatorum tuorum in terram proieci te, in conspectu regum dedi te dehonestari. *Propter multitudinem peccatorum tuorum et iniquitatem negotiationis tuae contaminavi sancta tua; educam ignem de medio tui, hic te devorabit. Et dabo te in cinerem in terra tua in conspectu omnium videntium te, et omnes qui te noverunt inter nationes contristabuntur super te: perditio factus es, et non eris in aeternum.*

Quoniam exaltatum est inquit *cor tuum, et dixisti: Deus sum ego, habitationem Dei habitavi in corde maris.* Et in hominem convenit *Ego sum Christus* et in diabolum, qui in corde maris, id est populi, habitat, sicut Deus in corde sanctorum suorum sedet. Populus in corde maris, id est in voluptate vel altitudine saeculi, habitat, sicut in alio loco dicit Deus eidem civitati: *Satiata et onerata es nimis in corde maris. In aqua multa deduxerunt te remiges tui; spiritus Austri contrivit te in corde maris virtutis tuae.*

Tu autem homo es, et non Deus. Et diabolus in homine homo dictus est, sicut Dominus dixit in Evangelio. *Inimicus homo hoc fecit,* et interpretatus est dicens: *Qui ea seminat diabolus est.* Homo diaboli Deus esse non potest. Propterea in utrumque convenit: *Tu homo es et non Deus.*

Dedisti cor tuum tamquam cor Dei. Numquid sapientior es tu Danihele? In Danihele totum corpus est Ecclesiae, quia non potest esse homo peccati sapientior in negotiis vitae, sicut ille *sapientior* est in suo *quam filii lucis.* Potest etiam in speciem convenire, quoniam Danihel specialiter confudit regem Babylonis in figura, qui prophetico Spiritu regem superbum ad confessionem unius Dei Ecclesiae maiestate prostravit, qui confessione

sinned; and you were stricken from the mountain of God. The cherubim drove you out from among the stones of fire. Your heart was puffed up at your splendor; your learning was corrupted through your splendor. For the multitude of your sins I have thrown you to the earth; I have disgraced you in the sight of kings. For the multitude of your sins and the evil dealings of your commerce I have defiled your sanctuary. I will bring fire from your midst; and it will consume you. I will turn you to ash in your land before the eyes of all who see you; and among the nations, all who know you will sorrow over you: you are ruined, gone for ever."[1]

"Your heart was puffed up," it says, "and you said: I am God, I dwelt in the dwelling of God in the heart of the sea."[2] The phrase, "I am the Christ,"[3] pertains both to man and to the devil, who dwells in the heart of the sea, i.e., of his people, just as God has his seat in the heart of his saints. The people dwell in the heart of the sea, i.e., in the desire or depth of this age, as God says to this same city in another passage: "you were too full and too heavily laden in the heart of the sea. Your oarsmen have brought you into deep water; the south wind has shattered you in the heart of the sea of your power."[4]

"You are a man and not god."[5] The devil, in a man, is also called a man, as when the Lord said in the gospel, "some man, an enemy, has done this," and went on to explain, "the one who sowed them is the devil."[6] A man belonging to the devil cannot be God. Therefore "you are a man and not God" applies to both.[7]

"You made yourself out to be the equal of God. Are you wiser than Daniel?"[8] In Daniel is represented the whole body of the church, for the man of sin[9] cannot be wiser in the commerce of life,[10] just as the man of sin is "wiser" in his own affairs "than are the children of light."[11] This can also pertain to the level of the particular, since, at the level of the particular, Daniel confounded the king of Babylon as a figure. By the prophetic Spirit, he brought the proud king to his knees to confess the one God by virtue of the church's majesty; by the confession of his own

---

[1]Ezek. 28:2-19

[2]Ezek. 28:2

[3]Mt. 24:5

[4]Ezek. 27:25-26

[5]Ezek. 28:2

[6]Mt. 13:28, 39

[7]That is, to both the devil and the person who belongs to the devil.

[8]Ezek. 28:2-3

[9]The allusion is to 2 Thess. 2:3.

[10]As opposed, that is, to the commerce of this world.

[11]Lk. 16:8

suarum virtutum et caelesti sapientia Babylonis superstitiones evertit.

Sapientes te non arguerunt sapientia sua? Non solum enim Danihel sapiens, sed etiam tres pueri, qui regem et omne regnum eius cum ipsis diis suis unum Dominum asserendo eiusdem Dei praesente virtute confuderunt. Idem nunc usque generaliter eiusdem tam externas quam intestinas Babylonis tenebras lumine veritatis disrumpunt.

Numquid in scientia tua aut sapientia tua fecisti tibi virtutem, et aurum et argentum thesauris tuis? Numquid in multa scientia et mercatu tuo multiplicasti tibi virtutem tuam, et exaltatum est cor tuum in virtute tua? Putant enim superbi et beneficiorum omnipotentis Dei ingrati sua virtute aliquid posse et sapientia ditari, nescientes scriptum esse: *Non levibus cursus, non fortibus proelium, neque sapienti panis.* Et iterum: *Numquid magnificabitur securis sine concisore?* Et non quidem prudentibus divitae, et non scientibus gratia. Haec enim non sunt in nostra potestate, sed a Deo conferuntur. *Quid enim habes quod non accepisti? Si autem accepisti, quid gloriaris tamquam non acceperis?* Et iterum: *Non glorietur sapiens in sapientia sua.*

Propterea haec dicit Dominus, Quoniam dedisti cor tuum sicut cor Dei, propterea ecce ego induco super te alienos, pestes ex gentibus, et exinanient gladios suos super te et super decorem scientiae tuae. Etsi potest in speciem convenire, quod reges saeculi per suam superbiam dominos se appelari patiuntur, tamen hoc quoque convenit in genus. Frequenter enim inducit Deus in Ecclesiam alienigenas, et multos in mortem vulnerant. Sed etiam occulta persecutione multos inducit ex gentibus, in quibus temptet populum suum, et occidat nequam partem simul cum eis sicut Maziam.

powers and his own heavenly wisdom, he overturned the superstitions of Babylon.[1]

"Have not the wise confuted you with their wisdom?"[2] For there was not only the wise man, Daniel, but also the three children, who confounded the king and all his kingdom, along with its very gods themselves, by affirming the one Lord in the present power of this same God.[3] Now, reaching out generally, they scatter the darkness of this same Babylon, both within and without, by the light of truth.

"Have you made yourself strong by your own knowledge or wisdom, or put gold and silver in your treasure houses? Have you multiplied your power in your great knowledge and your commerce, and has your heart swelled at your power?"[4] The proud and those who feel no gratitude for the benefits bestowed by almighty God think that they can accomplish things by their own strength and get rich by their own wisdom. They do not know that it is written: "the race does not go to the swift, nor the battle to the strong; nor is there bread for the wise."[5] And again: "will the axe get credit without the axeman?"[6] Nor does wealth go to the prudent or grace to those with knowledge.[7] For these things are not in our power, but are conferred by God. "For what do you have that you did not receive? And if you received it, why do you claim glory as if you had not?"[8] And again: "let not the wise man claim glory for his wisdom."[9]

"Therefore thus says the Lord: because you made yourself out to be the equal of God, behold, I am bringing foreigners against you, a bane from the nations; and they will draw their swords against you and against the splendor of your knowledge."[10] Although it is possible for this to pertain to the particular, since kings of this age in their pride do allow themselves to be called lords, it also pertains to the general. For God frequently leads foreigners against the church; and, on many, they inflict mortal wounds. But he also brings many from the nations as a kind of hidden persecution. Through them he puts his people to the test and puts the evil part to death along with them, as in the case of Zimri.[11]

---

[1]See Dan. 2:46-48.
[2]Ezek. 28:3
[3]See Dan. 3.
[4]Ezek. 28:4-5
[5]Eccles. 9:11
[6]Is. 10:15
[7]The allusion is to Eccles. 9:11.
[8]1 Cor. 4:7
[9]Jer. 9:23
[10]Ezek. 28:6-7
[11]See Num. 25.

Et vulnerabunt decorem tuum in perditionem. Aliquos enim non in perditionem sed cum spe sanitatis vulnerant. *Et deponent te,* id est humiliabunt, *et morieris morte vulnerato: m in corde maris.* Non diceret vulnerato *Morieris morte vulneratorum,* nisi quia non aperte vulneratur et moritur; sed ipse est, in quibus vulneratur.

Numquid narrabis in conspectu interficientium te: Deus sum ego? Id est numquid divini generis titulis terrebis eos quibus traditus fueris occidendus tam spiritaliter quam carnaliter? *Tu vero homo es et non Deus; in multitudine incircumcisorum peribis in manibus alienorum, quia ego locutus sum, dicit Dominus.* Nunc aperuit quo genere se ille dicat Deum, dum minatur et in multitudine incircumcisorum periturum manibus alienorum, quod non convenit nisi in eum qui sibi circumcisus videtur. Rex enim Tyri mortem solam potuit timere, non ne ab incircumcisis aut cum eis moreretur.

Et factus est sermo Domini ad me dicens: Fili hominis, accipe lamentum super principem Tyri, et dic illi: haec dicit Dominus, Tu es signaculum similitudinis, et corona decoris in paradiso Dei fuisti. Numquid diabolo factus est paradisus, ut ipse quod paradisum perdiderit increpetur? Homo fuit *in deliciis paradisi,* ipse est *signaculum similitudinis,* qui ad *similitudinem Dei* factus est. Signaculum autem ad decorem dixit, sicut per Aggeum dimicantibus huius adversum se fratribus promittit Deus Ecclesiae dicens: *Ego commovebo caelum et terram, mare et aridam. Et convertam currus et sessores, et descendent equi et sessores eorum unusquisque in gladio ad fratrem suum. In illo die, dicit Dominus omnipotens, accipiam te Zorobabel filium Salathiel servum meum, et ponam te signaculum, quoniam te elegi, dicit Dominus omnipotens.* Zorobabel omne corpus est, etenim exinde nusquam legimus commotis supra se universis venisse Zorobabel. Hic est autem ex tribus, qui sub Dario meruit aedificare Hierusalem. Ipse quoque in figura fundavit domum Dei et

"And they will wound your splendor to its ruin."[1] For they wound some people not to their ruin, but in the hope of healing them. "They will throw you down," i.e., humiliate you, "and you will die the death of the wounded in the heart of the sea."[2] There is no reason to tell one of the wounded, "you will die the death of the wounded," unless he is not visibly wounded and dying, but is himself present in those in whom he is wounded.

"Face to face with your murderers, are you still going to tell them: I am God?"[3] That is, are you still going to frighten them with claims to divinity when you are handed over to them to be killed both spiritually and physically? "In truth, you are a man and not God; you will perish at the hands of strangers in the throng of the uncircumcised, because I have spoken, says the Lord."[4] Now he has made it clear how it is that this fellow calls himself God. The threat that he will perish at the hands of strangers in the throng of the uncircumcised is only a threat to someone who counts himself circumcised. The king of Tyre might have feared death in its own right, but he would not have feared dying at the hands of the uncircumcised or among them.

"And the word of the Lord came to me and said: son of man, raise a lament over the prince of Tyre and say to him: thus says the Lord, you are a sign of likeness, and you were the crowning splendor in God's paradise."[5] Was paradise made for the devil so that he should be blamed for losing it? Man was the one who was "among the delights of paradise"; he is the "sign of likeness," made to "the likeness of God."[6] Now he called him a sign with respect to his splendor, just as in Haggai, when his brothers are fighting each other, God makes this promise to the church: "I am going to shake heaven and earth, sea and dry land. And I will overthrow the chariots and their riders; and the horses and their riders will fall, each by the sword of his brother. In that day, says the Lord almighty, I will take you, Zerubbabel son of Shealtiel, my servant; and I will make you a sign, for I have chosen you, says the Lord almighty."[7] Zerubbabel represents the whole body, for nowhere thereafter do we read that Zerubbabel came when men were stirred up against each other. Now this Zerubbabel is one of the three who, under Darius, gained the right to rebuild Jerusalem.[8] He also, in a figure, laid the

---

[1] Ezek. 28:7

[2] Ezek. 28:8

[3] Ezek. 28:9

[4] Ezek. 28:9-10. On the threat of being included among the uncircumcised, see also above, p. 75.

[5] Ezek. 28:11-13

[6] Gen. 5:1

[7] Hag. 2:21-23

[8] See 1 Esd. 3-4.

perfecit, sicut idem Dominus dixit: *Manus Zorobabel fundaverunt domum hanc, et manus eius perficient eam.* Quod est autem *signaculum* hoc et *corona speciei*, sic Deus promittit Ecclesiae dicens: *Videbunt gentes iustitiam tuam, et reges claritatem tuam, et vocabunt nomen tuum novum, quod Dominus nominabit illud. Eris corona speciei in manu Domini, et diadema regni in manu Dei tui. Tu etiam non vocaberis Derelicta, et terra tua non vocabitur Deserta; tibi enim nomen vocabitur Voluntas mea, et terra tua Orbis terrarum.* Homo est itaque *signaculum similitudinis* et *corona speciei*, cuius pars in ipso decore divinae similitudinis et *deliciis paradisi*, id est Ecclesiae, perseverat. Altera vero pars, *ne in aeternum vivat*, inter ipsam et arborem *flammeus ensis* evolvitur. *Adam* namque, sicut apostolus dicit, *umbra est futuri;* sic et in fratres divisus est in Cain et Abel.

Omnem lapidem optimum habens in te alligatum—sardium et topazium et smaragdum et carbunculum et saffirum et iaspin argentum et aurum et ligyrium et achaten et amethystum et chrysolithum et beryllum et onychinum—et auro replesti thesauros tuos et apothecas tuas in te. Haec et in diabolum conveniunt et in hominem. Isti enim duodecim lapides et aurum et argentum omnesque thesauri diabolo adhaerent delegati. Denique *habes in te alligatum*, et iterum *apothecas tuas in te*, sicut corpus Domini a sanctis ornatur, promittente Deo et dicente: *Extolle oculos tuos in circuitu et vide omnes filios tuos, collecti sunt et venerunt ad te. Vivo ego, dicit Dominus, quia omnibus illis indueris, et superimpones illos tibi sicut ornamentum novae nuptae; quia deserta tua et diruta et quae ceciderunt nunc angustiabuntur ab inhabitantibus.* Et in Apocalypsi eadem civitas duodecim lapidibus fundata construitur. *Omnem* inquit *lapidem optimum,* et enumeravit duodecim, ut ostenderet in duodenario numero perfectionem. Omnia enim quae fecit Deus bona sunt: horum diabolus usum non naturam mutavit. Et omnes homines excellentis sensus et potentis ingenii aurum sunt et argentum et lapides pretiosi secundum naturam, sed eius erunt in cuius obsequio voluntate non natura suis fruuntur, *quoniam cui se adsignaverit quis in obedientiam, servus est eius*

foundation of the temple of God and finished it, as the same Lord said, "Zerubbabel's hands laid the foundation of this temple, and his hands will finish it."[1] And what the "sign" is, that also is the "crowning splendor," as God promises to the church when he says, "the nations will see your righteousness and kings your glory; and they will call you by a new name, the name which the Lord will name. You will be a crowning splendor in the Lord's hand and a royal diadem in the hand of your God. No longer will you be called Forsaken, and your land will not be called Abandoned. For your name will be My Delight, and your land will be The World."[2] Man is therefore the "sign of likeness" and the "crowning splendor," of which a part perseveres in this splendor of the divine likeness and in "the delights of paradise," i.e., the church. But as for the other part, "lest it live for ever," a "flaming sword" turns about between it and the tree.[3] For "Adam," as the apostle says, "is a shadow of what is to come";[4] and so it is that he was divided into the brothers Cain and Abel.

"Set with every precious stone—carnelian and topaz and emerald and carbuncle and sapphire and jasper, silver and gold and jacinth and agate and amethyst and chrysolite and beryl and onyx—and you filled your treasure houses with gold and your storerooms within you."[5] These words pertain both to the devil and to man. For these twelve stones as well as gold and silver and all treasures, as assigned to the devil, adhere to him. Consequently it says, "set with," and again, "your storerooms within you." So too the Lord's body is adorned with the saints, as God promises when he says, "raise your eyes, look around and see all your children; they have been gathered and have come to you. As I live, says the Lord, you will wear all these and will put them on like the jewelry of a new bride, for your waste places and your devasted areas and your ruins will now be too small for their inhabitants."[6] In the Apocalypse, too, the same city is built on a foundation of twelve stones. "Every precious stone,"[7] he said, and he enumerated twelve in order to show perfect wholeness through the number twelve. For all things that God made are good; the devil has changed their use, but not their nature. Now all men of outstanding sense and powerful talent are gold and silver and precious stones by nature; but they will belong, by choice not by nature, to the one in whose service they find enjoyment in their powers. For anyone who consigns himself to another in obedience is the

---

[1]Zech. 4:9
[2]Is. 62:2-4
[3]Gen. 3:22, 24
[4]Rom. 5:14, apparently conflated with Col. 2:17.
[5]Ezek. 28:13
[6]Is. 49:18-19
[7]Rev. 21:19

cui obaudit, sive peccati sive iustitiae. Ita fit ut et diabolus habeat aurum et argentum et lapides pretiosos; omnia quidem non sua secundum originem, sed sua secundum voluntatem. Nam et in Iob scriptum est de diabolo: *Omne aurum maris sub eo est.* Et apostolus *vasa aurea et argentea* dicit esse *quaedam in contumeliam.* Non enim sicut quidam putant omnia *lignea* et *fictilia* reprobavit, cum ex eis sint aliqua in honorem, ipso dicente *figulum luti aliud quidem* fingere *in honorem aliud vero in contumeliam,* et ex ligno, aliud ad praeparationem escae aliud in sacrilegium. Ex auro et argento, id est ex magnis et perspicuis, dixit immundos. Nam et in Apocalypsi meretrix, id est corpus adversum, *purpura cocco et auro* et argento *lapidibusque pretiosis* ornatur, *habens poculum aureum in manu plenum execrationum et immunditiarum totius terrae.* Ista sunt ergo diaboli ornamenta, lapides pretiosi quibus *lapides igneos* imitatur.

Et homo in se habet thesauros tam facinorum quam perspicuos. Ipse enim suorum portator est, quem facultates suae velut compedes ligaverunt. Praeter illa quae ab utroque sexu corporis diaboli ornanda eduntur, etiam his quae defossa habent insitum est cor; *ubi enim erit thesaurus, illic erit et cor* hominis. Vetus enim homo et terra eius unum corpus est, quoniam ipse quoque terra est. Unde apostolus non solum ea, quae corpore admitti possunt, sed et avaritiam membrum esse possidentis ita definivit dicens: *Mortificate itaque membra vestra quae in terra sunt— fornicationem, immunditiam, passionem, concupiscentiam malam, et avaritiam, quae est idolorum servitus—propter quae venit ira Dei.*

Ex qua die creatus es tu cum cherubim imposui te in monte sancto Dei, id est in Christo vel in Ecclesia: *in medio lapidum igneorum fuisti,* id est hominum sanctorum, qui adunati montem Dei faciunt. Angeli enim alterius substantiae lapides dici non possunt, quia corpus non habent.

slave of the one he obeys, "either of sin or of righteousness."[1] So it happens that the devil also has his gold and silver and precious stones. None of these are his in virtue of their origin, but they are his in virtue of their choice. For in Job, too, it is written of the devil: "all the gold of the sea is under him."[2] And the apostle says that of the "dishes made of gold and silver" there are "some for ignoble use."[3] For it is not the case, as some think, that he repudiated all the dishes made of wood and clay. Some of these are for noble use, since he himself says that the potter shapes from "the clay, one thing for noble use, another for ignoble,"[4] and from wood, one thing for the preparation of food, another for sacrilege. It is from gold and silver, i.e., the great and the renowned, that he said the unclean come. For in the Apocalypse, too, the whore, i.e., the enemy body, is adorned with "purple, scarlet and gold" and silver "and precious stones, holding in her hand a gold cup full of the abominations and filth of all the earth."[5] These are, then, the devil's jewelry, the precious stones with which he imitates the "stones of fire."[6]

Man, also, has in himself treasures of lawlessness as well as of brightness. For he is the bearer of his own goods; his wealth has bound him like chains. Beyond these kinds of things, which are brought out for adornment by both sexes in the devil's body, the heart is also grafted to the things which they possess as buried deep in the earth. "For where his treasure is, there also is a man's heart."[7] For the old man and his earth are one body, since he also is of the earth.[8] This is why the apostle declared that not only the things which can be committed by the body, but also avarice is a member of the one who possesses it: "put to death, therefore, those of your members which are earthly—fornication, impurity, passion, evil desire, and avarice, which is the same as serving idols. On account of these, the wrath of God is coming."[9]

"From the day of your creation, I set you with the cherubim on God's holy mountain," i.e., in Christ or in the church; "you were among the stones of fire,"[10] i.e., among holy men who, joined as one, make up the mountain of God. For angels, being of another substance, cannot be called stones since they have no bodies. "You lived your days without blame

---

[1]Rom. 6:16
[2]Job 41:22 (cf. Septuagint)
[3]2 Tim. 2:20
[4]Rom. 9:21
[5]Rev. 17:4
[6]Ezek. 28:14
[7]Mt. 6:21
[8]The allusion is to 1 Cor. 15:47.
[9]Col. 3:5-6
[10]Ezek. 28:14

Abisti sine macula tu in diebus tuis ex qua die creatus es tu, donec invenirentur iniquitates tuae in te a multitudine negotiationis tuae. Lapides Ecclesiam dicit Petrus: *Et vos* fratres *tamquam lapides vivi coaedificamini domus spiritalis,* quam domum igneam esse et hanc in malos fratres ardere sic dicit Deus: *Erit domus Iacob ignis, domus autem Ioseph flamma, domus vero Esau stipula; et exardescent in illos et comedent eos, et non erit ignifer in domo Esau, quoniam Dominus locutus est.* Cum enim peccat homo, deicitur de monte Dei, et *non erit ignifer* amisso Spiritu, et succenditur *in cinerem.*

Peccasti et vulneratus es a monte Dei, et abduxit te cherubim de medio lapidum igneorum. Cherubim ministerium Dei est, quod exclusit universos malos de Ecclesia, sed spiritaliter. Qui enim *vestitum nuptialem* non habet, hic in saeculo excluditur de medio *recumbentium.* Denique *in tenebras,* id est in obdurationem, *mittitur,* donec in ignem aeternum descendat. Futuro enim saeculo nemo miscebitur choro sanctorum qui postea excludatur.

Exaltatum est cor tuum in decore tuo, corrupta est scientia tua in decore tuo. Corrupta est enim scientia eius qui sciens prudensque errat, et studio affectatae sapientiae asserit dissimulata veritate mendacium, sicut Spiritus dicit: *Cum cognovissent Deum, non ut Deum magnificaverunt aut gratias egerunt, sed nugati sunt in cogitationibus suis, dicentes se esse sapientes.* Corrupta est scientia eius qui alios docet, se ipsum non docet. Corruptus est decor eius qui generi suo operum similitudine non respondet.

from the day of your creation until your iniquities were discovered in you from the vastness of your commerce."[1] Peter calls the church stones: "and like living stones," brothers, "be yourselves built up as a spiritual house";[2] God calls this a house of fire and says that it will burn against the evil brothers: "the house of Jacob will be a fire, the house of Joseph a flame, and the house of Esau stubble. They will blaze out against them and consume them; and there will be nothing left to catch fire in the house of Esau, for the Lord has spoken."[3] When a man sins, he is cast down from the mountain of God; and "there will be nothing left to catch fire" once the Spirit has been lost, and he is burned "to ash."[4]

"You sinned and you were stricken from the mountain of God. The cherubim drove you out from among the stones of fire."[5] The cherubim represents the ministration of God, which has excluded all the evil from the church, but has done so spiritually. For the man who has no "wedding garment" is excluded from the wedding guests in this age. Accordingly "he is cast into the darkness,"[6] i.e., into obduracy, until he goes down into eternal fire. For, in the age to come, no one will mingle with the choir of the saints who will afterwards be excluded from it.[7]

"Your heart was puffed up at your splendor; your knowledge was corrupted through your splendor."[8] The person whose knowledge has been corrupted is the person who, for all his knowledge and good sense, still goes astray and, eager to affect wisdom, obscures the truth and asserts a lie, as the Spirit says: "although they knew God, they did not honor him as God or give him thanks, but became futile in their thinking even while claiming to be wise."[9] The person whose knowledge has been corrupted is the person who teaches others, but does not teach himself.[10] The person whose splendor has been corrupted is the person who does not respond to his origin by showing its likeness in his works.

---

[1]Ezek. 28:15-16

[2]1 Pet. 2:5

[3]Obad. 18

[4]Ezek. 28:18

[5]Ezek. 28:16

[6]Mt. 22:11, 13

[7]Tyconius' point is that Ezek. 28:16 refers to the exclusion of the evil from the church, but to the "spiritual" exclusion (i.e., the "obduracy" of inward disposition) that takes place in the present age rather than to the ultimate and total exclusion of the age to come when there will be no mingling at all of the evil with "the choir of the saints."

[8]Ezek. 28:17

[9]Rom. 1:21-22

[10]The allusion is to Rom. 2:21.

Propter multitudinem peccatorum tuorum in terram proieci te, in conspectu regum dedi te dehonestari. Et diabolus proiectus est in terram, id est in hominem, et homo de sublimitate Ecclesiae in conculcationem, sicut Hieremias dicit: *Deiecit de caelo in terram gloriam Israhel. In conspectu regum:* Christianorum dixit, quorum pedibus conculcatur diabolus et homo eius.

Propter multitudinem peccatorum tuorum et iniquitatem negotiationis tuae contaminavi sancta tua. Videtur veluti principalem titulum exprobrasse corpori diaboli negotiationes—magis dicit et thesauros—spiritalis nequitiae. Sicut enim spiritalis iustitiae negotiatio est thesaurus, ut Dominus dicit: *Simile est regnum caelorum homini negotiatori,* et iterum: *Thesaurizate vobis thesauros in caelo,* iterum *Dedit servis suis substantiam suam* ut negotiarentur, iterum *Negotiationes Carthaginenses* resistent tibi, iterum *Negotiatio eius et merces sancta Domino,* et apostolus *Est* inquit *negotiatio magna pietas;* ita spiritalis nequitia negotiatio est, thesaurus peccatorum, sicut Dominus dicit: *Homo malus de thesauro cordis emittit mala,* et apostolus: *Thesaurizas tibi iram in die irae.*

Propter iniquitatem inquit *negotiationis tuae contaminetur sancta tua.* Qui enim non recte sanctitate Dei utitur, suam efficit, sicut Deus dicit de sabbatis suis: *Sabbata vestra odit anima mea.*

Educam ignem de medio tui, hic te devorabit. Ignis Ecclesia est, quae cum discesserit e medio *mysterii facinoris* tunc pluet ignem Dominus a

"For the multitude of your sins, I have thrown you to the earth; I have disgraced you in the sight of kings."[1] The devil was thrown to the earth, i.e., into man; and the man was thrown down from the sublime height of the church to be trampled under foot, as Jeremiah says: "he has thrown down the glory of Israel from heaven to earth."[2] "In the sight of kings": he was speaking of Christians, under whose feet the devil and his man are trampled.

"For the multitude of your sins and the evil dealings of your commerce, I have defiled your sanctuary."[3] He seems to have made commercial transactions—indeed, he even speaks of storing up treasures—in spiritual wickedness the principal charge, as it were, against the devil's body. For commerce in spiritual righteousness is a storing-up of treasure, as the Lord says: "the kingdom of heaven is like a merchant";[4] and again: "store up treasures for yourselves in heaven";[5] again: "he entrusted his property to his servants"[6] so that they might use it in trade; again: "the merchants of Carthage"[7] will oppose you; again: "and her commerce and her profit will be holy to the Lord,"[8] and the apostle says, "there is great profit in godliness."[9] And in the same way, spiritual wickedness is a commerce, a storing-up of sins, as the Lord says, "the evil man brings forth evils from the treasure store of his heart,"[10] and the apostle: "you are storing up wrath for yourself on the day of wrath."[11]

"For the evil dealings of your commerce," he says, "your sanctuary is to be defiled."[12] For anyone who does not rightly use God's sanctity sets up a counter-sanctity of his own, just as God says of his sabbaths: "My soul hates your sabbaths."[13]

"I will bring fire from your midst; and it will consume you."[14] The fire is the church; and when it departs from the midst "of the mystery of

---

[1]Ezek. 28:17

[2]Lam. 2:1

[3]Ezek. 28:18

[4]Mt. 13:45

[5]Mt. 6:20

[6]Mt. 25:14

[7]Ezek. 38:13. "Carthage" is the Septuagint's reading.

[8]Is. 23:18

[9]1 Tim. 6:6

[10]Mt. 12:35

[11]Rom. 2:5

[12]Ezek. 28:18

[13]Is. 1:13, 14

[14]Ezek. 28:18

Domino de Ecclesia, sicut scriptum est: *Sol exortus est super terram, et Loth intravit in Segor. Et pluit Dominus super Sodomam et Gomorram sulphur et ignem a Domino de caelo.* Hic est ignis quem supra dixit: *Domus Iacob ignis, domus autem Esau stipula; et exardescent in eos et comedent illos, et non erit ignifer in domo Esau.* In Genesi iterum scriptum est: *Cum contereret Deus omnes civitates in circuitu, commemoratus est Deus Abrahae, et emisit Loth e medio subversionis, cum subverteret Deus civitates in quibus habitat in eis Loth.* Numquid Loth non merebatur propria iustitia liberari, ut diceret Scriptura: *Commemoratus est Deus Abrahae, et emisit Loth e medio subversionis?* Aut in civitatibus habitabat, et non in civitate, ut diceret: *Civitates in quibus Loth habitabat?* Sed prophetia est futurae discessionis. Memor enim Deus promissionis ad Abraham eiecit Loth de omnibus civitatibus Sodomorum, quibus veniet ignis ex igni Ecclesiae, quae de medio eorum educetur.

Et dabo te in cinerem in terra tua, id est in hominibus, vel ipsos homines in terra sua, qui in terra Dei esse noluerunt. *In conspectu omnium videntium te,* id est intellegentium. Numquid diabolus videri potest nisi in homine?

Et omnes qui te noverunt inter nationes contristabuntur super te. Cum enim Dominus percutit aut detegit malos, contristantur qui eorum auxilio fulciri solent, corporis sui parte debilitata.

Perditio facta es, et non eris in aeternum.

lawlessness,"[1] then the Lord will rain fire from the Lord down from the church, as it is written: "the sun rose over the land, and Lot entered Zoar. And the Lord rained brimstone and fire from the Lord down from heaven on Sodom and Gemorrah."[2] This is the fire which he mentioned above: "the house of Jacob will be a fire, and the house of Esau stubble. They will blaze out against them and consume them; and there will be nothing left to catch fire in the house of Esau."[3] In Genesis again, it is written: "when God laid waste all the cities of the area, God remembered Abraham and rescued Lot from the midst of the destruction when God destroyed the cities where Lot lived."[4] Was Lot's own righteousness not enough to warrant his rescue, so that scripture should say, "God remembered Abraham and rescued Lot from the midst of the destruction"? Or was Lot living in cities rather than in a city, so that it should say, "the cities where Lot lived"? But this is a prophecy of the departure to come. For God, remembering his promise to Abraham, plucked Lot from all the cities of Sodom, on which fire will come from the fire of the church, which will be taken from the midst of them.

"I will turn you to ash in your land,"[5] i.e., in men, or the men themselves in their land, the men who did not wish to be in God's land. "Before the eyes of all who see you,"[6] i.e., of all who understand. Can the devil be seen except in a man?

"And among the nations, all who know you will sorrow over you."[7] For when the Lord strikes down or unveils evil people, those who are accustomed to rely on their help for support are plunged into sorrow since a part of their own body is disabled.

"You are ruined, gone for ever."[8]

---

[1] 2 Thess. 2:7

[2] Gen. 19:23-24

[3] Obad. 18

[4] Gen. 19:29

[5] Ezek. 28:18. Tyconius takes the verse to apply either to the devil, who will be turned to ash in the men he inhabits, or to the men themselves, who will be turned to ash in their land (i.e., the land they have chosen rather than dwelling with God).

[6] Ezek. 28:18

[7] Ezek. 28:19

[8] Ezek. 28:19

SCRIPTURE CITATIONS AND ALLUSIONS

Old Testament and Apocrypha

---

*Allusions are distinguished by an asterisk.

148

New Testament